JAN 2 9 2003

5

Health Science Projects About Sports Performance

Robert Gardner and Barbara Gardner Conklin

Science Projects

Enslow Publishers, Inc.

40 Industrial Road   PO Box 38
Box 398   Aldershot
Berkeley Heights, NJ 07922   Hants GU12 6BP
USA   UK

http://www.enslow.com

S

*To Helen Marsh Sanford,
affectionately known as Honen,
whose zest for life inspired all who knew her.*

Library of Congress Cataloging-in-Publication Data

Gardner, Robert, 1929–
    Health science projects about sports performance / Robert Gardner and Barbara
Gardner Conklin.
        p. cm. — (Science projects)
        Includes bibliographical references and index.
        ISBN 0-7660-1441-X
        1. Sports—Physiological aspects—Experiments—Juvenile literature. 2. Human
physiology—Experiments—Juvenile literature. 3. Biology projects—Juvenile literature.
[1. Body, Human—Experiments. 2. Experiments. 3. Sports. 4. Science projects.]
    I. Conklin, Barbara Gardner. II. Title.
    RC1235 .G35   2002
    612'.044'078—dc21
                                                            2001006338

Printed in the United States of America

10 9 8 7 6 5 4 3 2 1

To Our Readers: We have done our best to make sure all Internet addresses in this book
were active and appropriate when we went to press. However, the author and the publisher
have no control over and assume no liability for the material available on those Internet sites
or on other Web sites they may link to. Any comments or suggestions can be sent by e-mail
to comments@enslow.com or to the address on the back cover.

Illustration credits: Stephen F. Delisle, pp. 15, 16, 17, 18, 21, 25, 27, 31, 44, 50,
57, 58, 59, 61, 62, 65, 69, 70, 80, 95, 96, 97; LifeART image copyright 1998
Lippincott Williams & Wilkins. All rights reserved, pp. 22, 55, 63, 67, 78.

Cover illustration: Jerry McCrea (foreground); © Corel Corporation
(background).

Contents

* appropriate ideas for science fair projects

* appropriate ideas for science fair projects

Introduction and Safety

The science projects and experiments in this book will lead you to investigate the effect of exercise and physical conditioning on heart rate, breathing rate, blood pressure, and body temperature. You can carry out experiments involving the muscles used in sports, perform tests to determine your physical condition, explore the psychological and nutritional aspects of sports and health, investigate ways to train for different sports, and learn how to warm up and stretch both before and after exercising.

To obtain data for some of the projects in this book you will need people to help you with experiments and serve as subjects. Because some experiments will take a significant amount of time, try to choose friends or family members who are patient and who enjoy experimenting as much as you do. Choose people who will commit to finishing these lengthy projects. Many of the projects will involve physical activity so be sure you and others participating in the projects are in good health and have a doctor's approval for vigorous exercise. Anyone with a health problem should not participate in projects involving exercise.

Like all good scientists, you will find it useful to record in a notebook your ideas, notes, data, and anything you can conclude from your experiments. By so doing, you can keep track of the information you gather and the conclusions you reach. Using your notebook, you can refer to experiments you have done, which may help you in doing future projects. In some of the experiments, you will have to make some calculations. Therefore, you may find it helpful to have a calculator nearby as you do these experiments and analyze the data you collect.

Science Fairs

Some of the projects in this book might be appropriate for a science fair. These projects are indicated with an asterisk (*). However, judges at science fairs do not reward projects or experiments that are simply copied from a book. For example, a model of a cell, which is commonly found at these fairs, would probably not impress judges unless it was done in a novel or creative way. A moving model of a muscle cell that demonstrates how such cells contract would receive more consideration than a rigid papier-mâché model.

Science fair judges seek to reward creative thought and imagination. However, it is difficult to be creative or imaginative unless you are really interested in your project. Therefore, choose something that appeals to you. Consider, too, your own ability and the cost of materials needed for the project.

If you decide to use a project in this book for a science fair, you will need to find ways to modify or extend it. This should not be difficult because as you do these projects new ideas for experiments will come to mind. It is these new experiments that will make excellent science fair projects because they spring from your own mind and are interesting to you.

If you decide to enter a science fair and have never done so before, you should read some of the books listed in the bibliography, including *Science Fair Projects—Planning, Presenting, Succeeding,* which is one of the books in this series. These books deal with science fairs specifically and will provide plenty of helpful hints and lots of useful information that will enable you to avoid the pitfalls that sometimes plague first-time entrants. You will learn how to prepare appealing reports that include charts and graphs, how to set up and display your work, how to present your project, and how to relate to judges and visitors.

Safety First

Most of the projects in this book are perfectly safe. However, some of them involve actions that could be dangerous. In these instances you will be reminded to work with a responsible adult. Read the following safety rules before you start any project.

1. Do any experiments or projects, whether from this book or of your own design, under the supervision of a science teacher or other knowledgeable adult.

2. Read all instructions carefully before proceeding with a project. If you have questions, check with your adult supervisor before going further.

3. Maintain a serious attitude while conducting experiments. Fooling around can be dangerous to you and to others.

4. Wear approved safety goggles when you are doing anything that might cause injury to your eyes.

5. Do not eat or drink while experimenting, unless instructed to do so.

6. Before anyone participates in any type of vigorous physical exercise, he or she should check with a doctor.

7. Check with a parent or a doctor before going on any diet.

8. Have a first-aid kit nearby while you are experimenting.

9. Do not put your fingers or any object in electrical outlets.

10. Many substances are poisonous. Do not taste anything unless instructed to do so.

1

Human History, Exercise, and Health

Humans were designed to be active. Our primitive ancestors were always in search of food and had to fight other predators for sustenance or take flight to safety. Our colonial ancestors also led active lives in order to survive. Physical work was a major part of the daily lives of farmers and pioneers in early America.

Automation and technology have lessened the need for physical labor. Although exercise is no longer an essential part of most of our lives, we need regular exercise to stay healthy. We no longer have to flee from woolly mammoths or fight for food, but our bodies still possess the "fight or flight" response. The stress we deal with is different than that of our ancestors, but the response to stress is the same. When we sense stress, the brain puts the body on full alert. There is an increased production of the stress-related hormones adrenaline and cortisol. In response to these hormones the heart beats faster, blood pressure rises, muscles become tense, and the body produces chemicals that are natural pain deflectors and performance enhancers. The pupils of the eyes dilate and hearing becomes more acute. The body is prepared for action, to fight or take flight.

If the stress does not require physical action, which is very often the case in modern society, our bodies are not relieved of the stress. Constant tension can make the muscles sore and rigid. Tight neck and shoulder muscles can make the head throb. Stomach acid secreted in response to stress can cause heartburn, cramps, and other digestive disorders. Instead of being "washed away" by physical activity, the chemicals released in the "fight or flight" response can accumulate in our bodies and interfere with our ability to fight infections. Other physical responses to stress include high blood pressure, fatigue, and an inability to sleep. Our bodies need physical activity to relieve stress and maintain health. If your lifestyle does not include regular physical activity, then you need an exercise program.

Exercise, such as walking, jumping, running, and playing sports, requires energy. Our bodies also need many different substances to maintain and grow tissues such as skin, bone, muscle, hair, and nails. The energy comes from the food we eat. For good health and to keep our bodies in working order, we need a regular supply of water and nutritious food. A balanced diet provides just the right amount of energy to fuel and maintain a healthy body.

Several body systems cooperate to provide our bodies with energy and movement. The digestive system turns the food we eat into the fuel we need for energy. Our respiratory system provides oxygen to release energy from the fuel. Our circulatory system carries the fuel and oxygen to all parts of our bodies. Our urinary, excretory, and respiratory systems remove waste materials from our bodies. Our skeletal and muscular systems provide support and allow our bodies to move.

No system in the human body works in isolation. Each system supports and is aided by all the others. When all these systems are in good working order, the body is healthy.

What is the definition of a healthy person? Some people might use physical features to describe a healthy person. Such terms might include "muscular" or "lean," but physical features are only part of good health. Good health requires a body that is strong enough to allow the person to perform daily tasks and to enjoy leisure activities, such as sports. There are four basic components of physical fitness that relate directly to a healthy body. They are cardiorespiratory fitness (a strong heart and lungs), flexibility, muscular strength and endurance, and body composition.

There are many advantages to being physically fit and healthy. These advantages include a lower risk of life-threatening heart disease or high blood pressure. In daily life physically fit people have better weight control, increased energy, and greater body flexibility and strength, meaning less chance of injury. They also often discover they have more self-confidence, clearer thinking, and a calmer response to stressful events.

2

Before Exercise: Warming Up and Stretching

Before participating in physical activity you should prepare your body for action. A warm-up provides the body with a period of adjustment between rest and physical activity. Warming up increases the heart rate and the internal body temperature. The increased blood supply to the muscles and the higher internal temperature help to loosen the muscles, making them more pliable, relaxed, and less subject to injury.

Many athletic injuries are related to poor flexibility. Flexibility is determined by the elasticity of the connective tissue around the joints. Strenuous exercise can increase muscle tightness and reduce flexibility. Stretching before and after exercising will increase flexibility and help to prevent injuries, stiffness, or pain following exercise. There is some controversy as to whether to stretch before or after exercise. Most experts recommend stretching both before *and* after any intense physical activity.

Before you do any stretching, you need to increase blood flow to your muscles. You can do this by means of a warm-up activity, such as marching, brisk walking, or light jogging. You should warm up for at least five minutes. After the warm-up, stretch your muscles, concentrating on the ones you are going to use most during the physical activity. For example, if you are going to run, you should focus on your legs and feet. We suggest stretching all major muscle areas. Just a few stretches of all major muscles will prepare your body for any action and help with flexibility.

When you do a stretch, never bounce. Bouncing can cause a muscle to contract at the same time it is being stretched, which will reduce the effectiveness of the stretch and possibly cause muscle soreness. Instead, move gently into the stretch and then hold the position. Breathe naturally as you stretch. Do not hold your breath.

After you have completed your physical activity, you need to cool your body to prevent injury and muscle soreness. A cool-down is done in much the same way as the warm-up. Slow your activity to light jogging or brisk walking until your breathing and heart rate are no longer elevated. Then stretch your muscles again.

If the exercise you plan to do requires considerable use of certain parts of the body, you should do additional stretches to those areas before and afterward.

After you have warmed up, do the following stretches in the order presented. When you are finished exercising and cooling down, do the same stretches. Repeat each stretch a few times.

Stretching Head and Neck

- Standing straight with knees slightly bent, lower your right ear toward your right shoulder, then raise your head to look forward. Do not roll your head back to look upward because this puts stress on the cervical vertebrae at the top of your spine. Lower your chin to your chest, then raise it. Do the same stretch for the left side.

- Turn your head to look over your right shoulder, then your left.

- Rotate your head in half circles to the right and to the left.

Stretching Shoulders and Arms

- Put your right forearm behind your head, as if you are trying to reach a zipper. Grab your right elbow with your left hand and gently pull the elbow behind your head until you feel slight tension in your right arm. Hold for a few seconds. Repeat on the other arm.

- Put one arm across your chest at shoulder height. With your other hand, push the arm at the elbow into your body and hold. Repeat with the opposite arm.

- Slowly roll your shoulder joints in circles, both forward and backward. Then do circles with elbows bent and upper arms circling with the shoulders (Figure 1a). Finally do full, slow vertical circles with your arms (Figure 1b).

Stretching Waist

- Standing with your feet shoulder-width apart, left hand on left hip and right hand extended above your head, bend slowly at the waist to the left. Hold at the first point you feel tension in your waist. Repeat on the other side.

Stretching Legs

- Lean over, placing your hands on the ground, with one leg bent at the knee at a right angle to the ground and your chest resting lightly on that thigh. Stretch your other leg behind. Press your hips down until you feel tension in the back leg. Alternate legs. (See Figure 2a).

- From the above lunge position, straighten the front leg and put your weight on the back leg. Flex the front foot back and reach over the front leg with your body (Figure 2b). You should feel stretching in the back leg. Alternate sides.

- Standing on your right leg, reach back and grab your left foot. Lift the heel of that foot to the buttock. Hold for a few seconds.

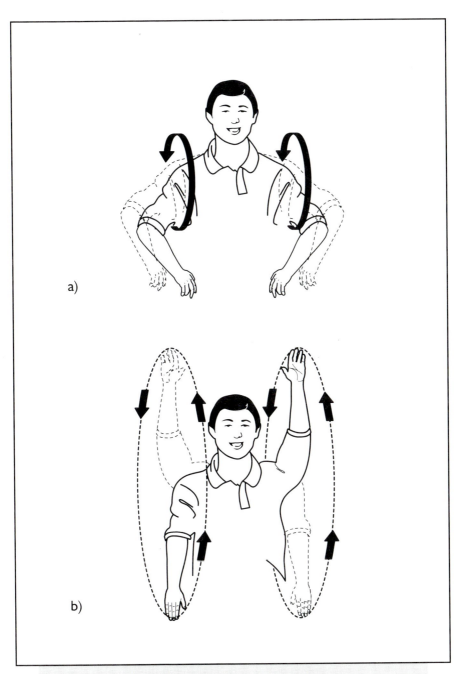

Figure 1. Stretching the arms and shoulders.

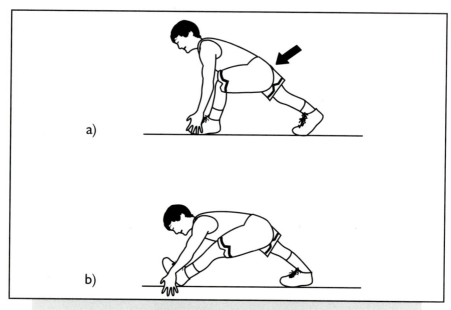

Figure 2. Stretching the legs.

You should feel the stretch in the front of the left thigh. Alternate legs (Figure 3).

- Stand an arm's length from a wall. Put your hands on the wall. Slide one foot back about two feet. Keeping both heels flat on the floor, bend the front leg and lean forward, straightening the back leg to stretch the calf muscle. Hold a few seconds. Alternate legs.

- Sit with both legs extended in front of you. Reach toward the toes and hold. You will feel stretching in the back of your legs and your lower back.

- Still sitting, bring your feet toward your body. Place the soles of your feet together. Hold your ankles and use your elbows to press on the inside of both knees. Press the knees down and hold (Figure 4). You will feel stretching in the groin.

- Sit with one leg tucked into the body and the other leg extended. Reach forward and try to touch the toes of the

Figure 3. Stretching the thigh muscles.

extended leg. You will feel stretching in the tucked leg. Hold, then alternate legs.

Stretching Back

- Lie on your back. Bend one leg and hold it under the knee. Keep the other leg straight and on the ground. Hug the knee to your chest. Alternate. Then bring both knees into your chest and roll your head up to meet the knees. Hold for a few seconds. You will feel stretching in your lower back.

- While on your hands and knees, arch your back toward the ceiling like a cat would. Hold a few seconds, then relax your back until it is parallel with the floor. You will feel stretching in your middle and lower back.

- Slowly go into a standing position. While doing so, bend your knees and arch your back down as you place your hands on your thighs to support your back. Roll your back up until you are standing with your shoulders back. You will feel a nice stretch in your back and shoulders.

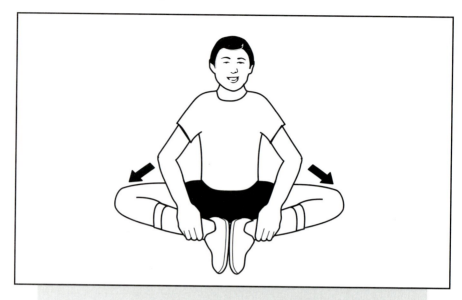

Figure 4. Stretching the legs and groin.

Stretching the Whole Body

- Stand erect with the fingers of both hands intertwined in front of you. Lift your arms overhead as you turn your palms outward. Lift onto your toes and slowly let your arms reach to the sides and down as you come down off your toes. This is a good way to end your stretching. You will feel stretching from your toes all the way up through your back to the shoulders, arms, and fingers.

- Repeat stretching exercises in reverse order, if you like.

3

Some Necessary Tools and Skills

Some experiments presented in this book require the use of some common medical instruments and skills. The instruments, which are not expensive, may be available in your home or at your school's science or medical department.

The following experiments are designed to help you learn how to use the instruments and develop the skills needed to measure heart rate, breathing rate, body temperature, and blood pressure. These measurements provide doctors and nurses with what are known as vital signs.

Being familiar with these tools and skills will enable you to carry out experiments to find out how exercise and physical conditioning affect heart rate, breathing rate, body temperature, and blood pressure.

3-1
Measuring Heart Rate

Usually you can't feel your heart beat. After vigorous exercise, or if you are scared, you can feel it. You can, however, always determine your heart rate by taking your pulse.

Things you will need:
• a volunteer
• clock or watch with a second hand
• stethoscope

Each time your heart beats it forces blood into your arteries. The added blood swells the elastic walls of the large arteries near your heart, sending a pulse of expansion along the walls of those arteries. It is much like the movement of a wave along a rope or slinky. The expansion of the radial artery, on the underside of the wrist, can be felt every time the heart beats. It is where doctors and nurses take your pulse. To feel a pulse, place your two middle fingers on the inside of your own or a volunteer's wrist, as shown in Figure 5. Can you feel the pulse?

Now that you know how to take a pulse, use a watch or clock with a second hand to measure your heart rate (number of beats per minute). Count the number of heart beats over a thirty-second period. Multiply this number by two to obtain your heart rate in beats per minute. What is your heart rate? What is the heart rate of your volunteer? What are the heart rates of the people in your family?

A pulse can be felt on any artery that is close to the body's surface. For example, you can feel the pulsing of the carotid arteries in your neck on either side of your Adam's apple (larynx). You can also feel (and sometimes see) the pulse of the temporal artery just in front of your ear. In what other places on your body can you find a pulse? If you find a pulse at a point on the left side of your body, can you always find a pulse on the corresponding point on the right side?

If you take your volunteer's pulse at both the neck and the wrist, which pulse do you expect to feel first? Try it! Were you right?

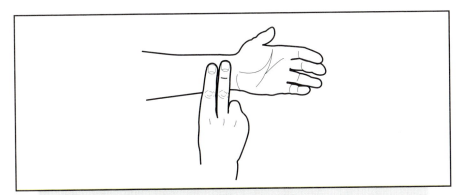

Figure 5. To take a pulse place your middle finger and index finger on the underside of the subject's wrist, just behind the thumb, as shown.

Measuring Heart Rate with a Stethoscope

To hear how each throb of a pulse is caused by a contracting heart, use a stethoscope to listen to your volunteer's heart while taking his or her pulse. Place the stethoscope's ear tips in your ears and the chest piece slightly to the left of the center of the person's chest. Move the chest piece slightly until you hear the heart sounds clearly. Listen for two sounds in close succession. The first is a relatively long booming sound. The second is a short, sharp sound. Together they make a "lubb-dup" sound. The "lubb" is caused by the contracting muscle and the closing of the valves between the heart's chambers (the ventricles and atria). The "dup" is the sound made by the closing of the valves between the heart and the two major arteries into which blood is pumped (the aorta and the pulmonary artery). These arteries and valves can be seen in the diagram of the heart shown in Figure 6.

If you don't have a stethoscope, you can hear heart sounds by placing your ear against your volunteer's chest.

Where would you place the chest piece of a stethoscope to hear blood flowing through a person's carotid arteries? Can you hear the blood flowing through these arteries that lead to the head?

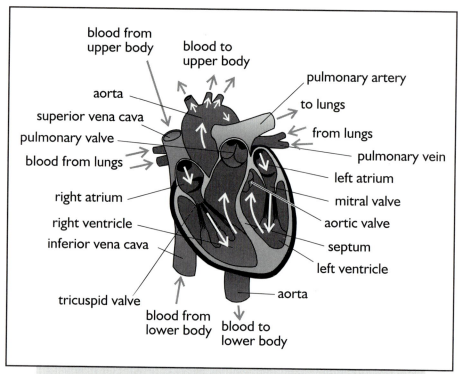

Figure 6. A schematic drawing of the heart shows its four chambers. They consist of the right and left atria and the right and left ventricles. The diagram also shows the main veins carrying blood to the heart—the superior and inferior vena cava and the pulmonary veins—as well as the two main arteries carrying blood from the heart—the aorta and the pulmonary artery. Shown, too, are the aortic valve, the pulmonary valve, and the valves between the auricles and ventricles—the tricuspid valve and the mitral valve.

3-2
Measuring Breathing Rate

Have your volunteer lie on his back on a couch or floor. Watch his chest move up slightly each time he inhales. Using a watch or clock with a second hand determine how many times he breathes in one minute. What is the person's breathing rate? What is your breathing rate?

Things you will need:
- a volunteer
- clock or watch with a second hand
- an adult
- paper bag

How can you measure your volunteer's breathing rate if he is standing?

Can you think of another way to measure your volunteer's breathing rate?

As you probably know, some of the oxygen in the air you inhale is transferred from your lungs to your blood. At the same time, some of the carbon dioxide in your blood passes into the air in your lungs. As a result of this exchange of gases, exhaled air has less oxygen and more carbon dioxide than inhaled air.

What do you predict will happen to your breathing rate and depth of breathing if you breathe the same air over and over again? **Under adult supervision**, you can find out by placing the open end of a paper bag tightly around your nose and mouth. Breathe and rebreathe the air in the bag for a minute or two. What happens to your breathing rate? What happens to your depth of breathing (the volume of air you take into your lungs with each breath)? How can you explain the changes in breathing you observe?

3-3
Measuring Blood Pressure

Pressure is defined as force per area (force ÷ area). The pressure you exert on the floor is your weight divided by the area of your shoes touching the floor. Blood pressure is the force that

blood exerts against the surface area of blood vessel walls. Blood pressure in arteries is greatest when the heart is contracting, forcing more blood into these vessels. It is lowest when the heart is between pumps.

Blood pressure involves two measurements, systolic pressure and diastolic pressure. Systolic pressure is the larger one. It occurs when the heart contracts, pushing blood into the arteries. Diastolic pressure appears just before the heart contracts, when the pressure in the arteries is at a minimum.

The systolic pressure is recorded first, followed by the diastolic pressure. A normal record of blood pressure might read 120/70. The pressures are measured in millimeters (mm) of mercury. The pressure of the earth's atmosphere at sea level, which we measure with a barometer, is normally 760 mm of mercury. This means the air can support a column of mercury 760 mm high, which is the same pressure as 10.1 newtons per square centimeter, or 14.7 pounds per square inch. Of course, blood, like the rest of your body, is subject to air pressure. Consequently, blood pressure is the pressure by which the blood's pressure in arteries exceeds that of the air.

Pulse pressure is the difference between systolic and diastolic blood pressure. In the example given above, the pulse pressure would be:

$$120 - 70 = 50 \text{ mm of mercury}$$

The easiest way to measure blood pressure is with a battery-operated monitor that fits over a person's index finger or wrist.

24

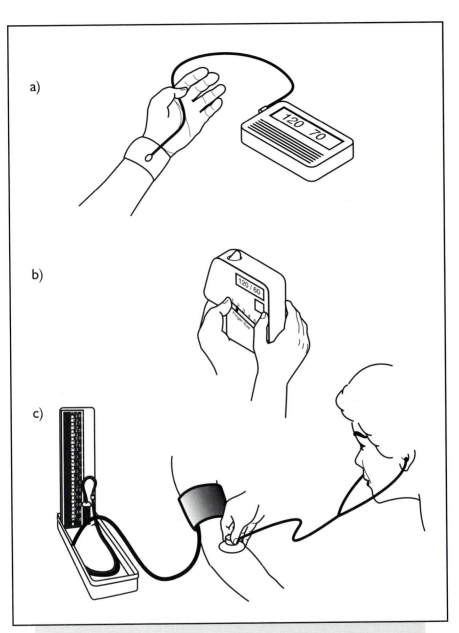

Figure 7. These devices are used to measure blood pressure. a) An automatic cuff-type blood pressure and pulse monitor. A similar model fits over the upper arm. b) A finger-type automatic blood pressure and pulse monitor. c) A sphygmomanometer, such as those commonly found in a doctor's office.

It provides a digital display of both systolic and diastolic pressure. Still another battery-powered blood pressure monitor inflates at the press of a button and gives a digital display of blood pressure and pulse rate. Your family may have an instrument similar to one of those shown in Figure 7a or 7b. If not, you may be able to borrow one from a friend or from your science teacher or school nurse.

The more traditional device for measuring blood pressure is the sphygmomanometer (Figure 7c) found in doctors' offices. A sphygmomanometer is more difficult to operate than the automatic devices. It consists of a cuff that is placed around the upper arm and then inflated. When the pressure in the cuff exceeds the pressure of the blood flowing through the brachial artery in the upper arm, the artery collapses and blood flow stops. By slowly reducing the pressure in the cuff, a point is reached at which systolic pressure forces a spurt of blood through the artery. The short spurt of blood produces a sound that can be heard by placing a stethoscope over the artery below the cuff on the inside of the elbow. When the first sound is heard, the pressure is read on a gauge attached to the cuff. As the pressure in the cuff continues to be slowly reduced, the sound becomes more muffled and eventually disappears when the cuff no longer restricts blood flow. Consequently, the pressure at which the sound disappears is the subject's diastolic blood pressure.

If possible, use one of the automatic blood pressure devices. Should you have to use a sphygmomanometer, **ask an adult** familiar with taking blood pressure to help you. **Be sure that the cuff does not restrict a subject's blood flow for more than a few seconds.**

Ask your volunteer to sit in a chair with her arm on a table. Determine her blood pressure with whichever instrument is available. What is her systolic blood pressure? What is her diastolic blood pressure? What is her pulse pressure?

Now, reverse roles. What is your blood pressure? What is your pulse pressure?

3-4
Measuring Body Temperature

The temperature of a person's body can be determined with an oral thermometer such as one of those seen in Figure 8. If you use a mercury thermometer, ask

Things you will need:
* oral thermometer
* parent, nurse, or teacher
* a few volunteers

a parent, nurse, or science teacher to show you how to shake down the column of liquid until the mercury reading is below 35°C, or 95°F. If you are using a mercury thermometer, place the thermometer under your tongue for three minutes and then remove it and read the temperature. Most digital thermometers will use a sound signal to indicate when the temperature has reached its maximum value and is no longer changing.

Use an oral thermometer to measure your body temperature. What is it?

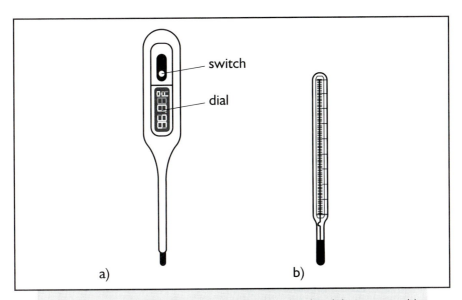

switch

dial

a)

b)

Figure 8. Body temperature may be measured with a digital thermometer (a) or a mercury thermometer (b).

After you use it, clean the thermometer with cotton soaked in rubbing alcohol. After the thermometer has dried, use it to measure someone else's body temperature. Is that person's temperature the same as yours? If not, does one of you have a fever?

Measure the body temperatures of a few healthy volunteers. Are they all the same? If not, by how many tenths of a degree do they differ? Do you agree with the statement, "Normal body temperature is 37°C, or 98.6°F"?

4

The Effects of Body Position, Exercise, and Conditioning

How does body position affect heart rate, breathing rate, body temperature, and blood pressure? Does your heart beat faster when you stand up? Does exercise affect these vital signs? Can physical conditioning change the way heart rate, breathing rate, body temperature, and blood pressure respond to changes in body position or to exercise? The experiments found in this chapter will help you answer these and other questions.

4-1
The Effect of Body Position, Exercise, and Conditioning on Heart Rate

Things you will need:

• clock or watch with second hand

• a partner

• notebook and pen or pencil

• a volunteer who is in very good physical condition

• a volunteer who is not in very good physical condition

• graph paper

(To save time, you can combine this experiment with the next two experiments.) You will need three partners. Have one partner measure heart rate, while another measures breathing rate, and a third takes the subject's blood pressure. In this way, the data for three experiments can be obtained at the same time. If you have a blood pressure monitor that also records heart rate, you will only need two partners.

Lie on your back on a couch or floor and rest quietly for five minutes. Then have your partner take your pulse to determine your heart rate. Record that number in your notebook.

Sit up for five minutes. Again, have your partner take your pulse, then record the number in your notebook. Is your heart rate higher while you are sitting?

Now, stand for five minutes. Again, have your partner determine your heart rate, and record the result. Does your heart beat faster while you are standing?

Run in place for five minutes. As soon as you stop running, stand still as your partner takes your pulse. After recording your heart rate, have your partner take your pulse and record your heart rate at one-minute intervals until it returns to the rate you had when standing before exercising.

Plot a graph of your heart rate in beats per minute versus time, in minutes, for the period following your exercise. One such graph is shown in Figure 9. How does it compare with the graph you made? What can you conclude from the graph you made?

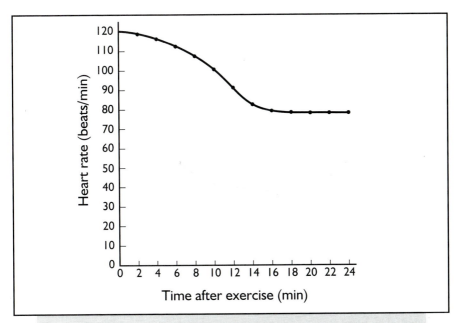

Figure 9. This graph shows a person's heart rate versus time, in minutes, after exercise. How does it compare with the graph you made?

Repeat this experiment with a volunteer who is in very good physical condition and with a volunteer who is not. (See Experiment 7-1 for tests to determine physical condition.) How do the data for the two volunteers compare?

4-2
The Effect of Conditioning and Exercise on Breathing Rate

Lie on your back on a couch or floor and rest quietly for five minutes. After that time, your partner will watch your chest to determine how many times you breathe in one minute. Record that data in a notebook. What is your breathing rate while lying on your back?

Things you will need:

- clock or watch with second hand
- a partner
- notebook and pen or pencil
- a volunteer who is in very good physical condition
- a volunteer who is not in very good physical condition
- graph paper

Sit up and remain seated for five minutes. Again, have your partner determine your breathing rate after that time. Record the data. What is your breathing rate while sitting?

Stand up for five minutes and then have your partner determine your breathing rate. Record the data. What is your breathing rate when standing?

Next, run in place for five minutes. As soon as you stop running, stand still as your partner counts the number of breaths you take in fifteen seconds. How can that data be recorded as breaths per minute?

In the same way, have your partner determine your breathing rate at one-minute intervals until your breathing rate returns to the rate you had when standing before exercising. Record all the data.

Plot a graph of breathing rate in breaths per minute versus time, in minutes, for the period following your exercise. What can you conclude from the graph?

Repeat this experiment with a volunteer who is in very good physical condition and with a volunteer who is not. (See Experiment 7-1 for tests to determine physical condition.) How do the data for the two people compare?

4-3*
The Effect of Conditioning and Exercise on Blood Pressure

Things you will need:

- a partner
- battery-powered automatic blood pressure device or sphygmomanometer and stethoscope
- pen or pencil
- notebook
- clock or watch
- graph paper

Lie on your back on a couch or floor and rest quietly for five minutes. After that time, have your partner measure your blood pressure while you are still on your back. Record both your diastolic and systolic pressure. What is your blood pressure while lying on your back?

Next, sit up and remain seated for five minutes. While you are seated, have your partner measure your blood pressure. Record the data. What is your normal blood pressure while sitting?

Now, stand for five minutes. Have your partner measure your blood pressure as you stand. Record the data. What is your blood pressure while standing? What is your pulse pressure?

Next, run in place for five minutes. As soon as you stop running, stand still as your partner measures your blood pressure. Record that data in your notebook. What is your blood pressure immediately after exercising? What is your pulse pressure?

While you are standing, have your partner measure your blood pressure at three-minute intervals until your blood pressure is nearly the same as it was when standing before exercising. Record the data. Use that blood pressure data to plot a graph of blood pressure versus time after exercising. Use the same data to plot a graph of pulse pressure versus time after exercise. What can you conclude from these graphs?

Repeat this experiment with a volunteer who is in very good physical condition and with a volunteer who is not. (See Experiment

7-1 for tests to determine physical condition.) How do the data for the two people compare?

Exploring on Your Own

Measure the breathing, heart rates, and blood pressures of a number of different people after they have been lying, sitting, standing, and exercising for five minutes. Does a subject's age, weight, gender, or physical condition seem to affect the results? If so, how are the results related to these factors?

4-4*
The Effect of Conditioning and Exercise on Body Temperature

Things you will need:

Before you begin this experiment, do not exercise for at least an hour. Use an oral thermometer to measure your body temperature. Place the thermometer under your tongue for three minutes. What is your body tem-

- place where you can exercise, such as a gymnasium or yard
- oral thermometer
- household thermometer
- vacuum cleaner

perature after you have been lying down for five minutes? What is your body temperature after sitting for five minutes? After standing for five minutes?

Now run in place for five minutes or until you are perspiring freely. Take your temperature again. Record your temperature at five-minute intervals. How long did it take before your temperature was the same as it was before exercising? Did your temperature change significantly after exercising? How much did it change? Can you explain why?

Now, compare your change in temperature with that of a machine, such as a vacuum cleaner. A vacuum cleaner pulls in air that passes through a filter (bag), over the motor, and out an opening at the back or top of the machine. To begin this part of the experiment, place a household thermometer at the opening where air emerges from the vacuum cleaner. What is the temperature at the opening? Continue to hold the thermometer in place as you turn on the vacuum cleaner. What happens to the temperature of the air coming out of the machine? Does the temperature become constant after the motor has run for some time? Why or why not?

How did the change in temperature of the air coming out of the vacuum cleaner compare with your temperature change following exercise? Can you explain any differences in these two temperature changes?

Exploring on Your Own

Do some research at a library or on the Internet to find out how body temperature is controlled.

Explain how a vacuum cleaner works. What must happen for it to pull in air?

4-5*
Effect of Temperature on the "Breathing" Rate of a Fish

Fish don't breathe as we do. They gulp water that they force through their gills, causing the gill flaps to open. As the water passes through the gills, it comes in contact with a rich supply of capillaries carrying blood. Some of the oxygen dissolved in the water is transferred to the fish's blood and some of the carbon dioxide in the blood enters the water. This exchange of gases is very similar to the exchange between air and blood that takes place in our lungs when we breathe.

Things you will need:

• goldfish

• fish bowl or tank

• filtered ice water

• filtered hot water

• household thermometer

• watch or clock with a second hand

If you watch a goldfish in a bowl or tank from above, you can see the gill flaps, just behind its eyes, open at regular intervals. To measure the fish's respiration rate, count the number of times its gill flaps open in 15 seconds. Then multiply by 4 to obtain its respiration rate in "breaths" per minute.

To find out how water temperature affects the animal's respiration rate, you can change the temperature of the water in the bowl or tank by very slowly and carefully adding ice water or hot water as you stir with a household thermometer. The water temperature should not change by more than 5°C (10°F) between the times you measure the fish's respiration rate. Allow about 5 minutes for the goldfish to adjust to its new environment before determining its respiration rate. **Never raise the water temperature above 35°C (95°F) or lower it below 13°C (55°F).**

How does temperature affect the fish's respiration rate? What other factors might have affected the respiration rate of the fish? How might you control those factors?

Exploring on Your Own

Design and carry out an experiment to find out how temperature affects the breathing rate of humans. If breathing rate is related to temperature, does it also depend on weight? On gender? On age?

4-6
Maintaining Body Temperature

As you found in Experiment 4-4, your temperature does not change very much. Even when the heat of summer raises air temperatures above 100°F (38°C), your body temperature changes very little.

How can your temperature remain nearly constant even when the air around you is warmer than your body? Sitting in front of an electric fan will help to keep you cool. But does the fan cool the air?

To find out, hang a household thermometer near the center of the room to measure the temperature of the still air. After a few minutes, read and record the temperature. Next, turn on the fan. Watch the thermometer. Does the air get cooler?

Things you will need:

* electric fan
* household thermometer
* small cotton cloth
* rubber bands
* tape
* plastic bag larger than your hand
* aluminum foil
* eyedropper
* water
* rubbing alcohol
* cooking oil
* light, loose clothing
* bathroom scale
* towel
* a dark shirt and a white shirt

If a fan does not cool the air, there must be some other reason it makes you feel cooler. Dip a small piece of cotton cloth into some lukewarm water. Then squeeze out the excess water. Wrap the cloth around the lower end of the thermometer. The cloth should completely cover the thermometer's bulb. Use a rubber band to hold the cloth in place. When the liquid in the thermometer stops moving, read and record the temperature. Then hang the thermometer in the wind generated by the fan. What happens to the temperature?

Leave the thermometer in front of the fan until the cloth is dry. What is the temperature when the cloth is thoroughly dry? How

39

does it compare with the temperature of the air in the room when the fan is turned off?

What causes the temperature of the wet cloth to decrease? To find out, spread a few drops of water on the back of one of your hands. Leave the other hand dry. Hold both hands in the moving air coming from a fan. Which hand feels cooler?

Repeat the experiment when both hands are dry. Do both hands feel about the same now?

You may have seen a wet road or sidewalk become dry after a rainstorm. The water evaporates; it changes from a liquid to a gas. You may also have noticed that the water evaporates faster when a wind is blowing. The same thing happened to the water on your hand when you held it near the fan.

Water, like all substances, is made up of molecules. These tiny particles of matter move faster when they are heated. The higher the temperature, the faster they move. The water molecules on your hand absorbed heat from your body. As they did, the faster moving ones escaped into the air and were carried away by the wind from the fan, leaving the slower (cooler) ones behind to absorb more heat from your body.

Normally, when you are hot, you perspire. The sweat absorbs heat from your body as it evaporates. This helps keep your body cool. If the wind is blowing, sweat evaporates faster from your body and you feel even cooler. What happens when the air is very humid; that is, when there is a lot of moisture in the air? To find out you can do some other experiments.

A Hand in a Bag

Put one of your hands inside a plastic bag. Use tape to seal the mouth of the bag around your wrist. Then go for a run. As you begin to sweat, which hand feels warmer? What do you see collecting on the inside surface of the plastic bag? How can you explain your observation?

Later, when you are cool and at rest, cover your hand with another plastic bag. Seal it as before and continue to wear it for an hour or so while you read or sit quietly. At the end of this period, carefully examine the bag on your hand. What evidence do you have that water evaporates from your body even when you are at rest?

Perspiration and Weight

You have seen that water in the form of perspiration appears on your skin when you exercise. Exercise requires energy, and much of the energy is released as heat, which tends to raise your body temperature. Your body responds by forming beads of perspiration that evaporate and cool your body. But how much weight do you lose by sweating?

For this experiment, be sure you are fully hydrated. Drink a pint (two large glasses) of water two hours before exercising and another glass of water half an hour before exercising. Put on light, loose clothing and then weigh yourself. Record your exact weight in your notebook.

Exercise vigorously for at least half an hour. You might run, play a competitive game of basketball, do calisthenics, or engage in any other form of exercise that will make you perspire. After exercising, dry yourself thoroughly with a towel before weighing yourself again. Record your weight. How much weight did you lose? What percentage of your body weight did you lose?

If possible, repeat this experiment under different weather conditions. How does your weight loss on a cool, dry day compare with your weight loss on a hot, humid day? How about on a dry, hot day?

5

Nutrition and Health

During the last decade obesity in the United States has increased by 60 percent. Nearly one fifth of the people in this country are now classified as obese (fat) and one third are overweight (weigh more than is normal). Being overweight can lead to heart disease, diabetes, and other physical problems. Consequently, it makes good sense to exercise and eat right.

Participating in sports is one good way to exercise and have fun at the same time. However, excess weight requires the heart to pump harder and faster to supply all the extra flesh with blood. Consequently, exercise should be accompanied by proper nutrition. A healthy diet includes fruits, vegetables, grains, low-fat dairy products, fish, and lean meat. Junk food, which is often rich in fats, sugar, and salt, should be avoided.

In this chapter you will find basic information about how we use food in our bodies. You will also learn how to perform simple tests to find out if you are overweight.

5-1
Basal Metabolism

Metabolism is the body's use of food after it has been digested and transported to cells. Our body cells use food as a source of energy and as raw materials for building the complex molecules we need to live.

Things you will need:
- a few volunteers
- Table 1 and Figure 10
- calculator (optional)

Metabolic rate is the speed at which our bodies release the energy stored in food. It is usually expressed as Calories per hour (Cal/h) or Calories per day (Cal/day)

A person's basal metabolic rate (BMR) is the rate at which energy must be produced just to keep the body alive. It is measured when the subject is awake, lying down, and at rest in a warm room, 12 to 18 hours after eating any food. The rate can be measured directly by placing the subject in a chamber where the heat is calculated by the change in temperature of water that is circulated through the chamber. Heat released by the body warms the water. By knowing the amount of water and its temperature change, the heat released by the body can be calculated.

BMR can also be determined indirectly by measuring the volume of oxygen (O_2) consumed and carbon dioxide (CO_2) produced per hour by a subject. Scientists have found the volume of CO_2 divided by the volume of O_2 can be used to determine the energy released.

From direct measurements, we know that a person's BMR depends on surface area; that is, the area of the skin that covers the body. The larger a person's surface area, the more heat that is lost to the cooler air surrounding the body. To keep the body temperature constant, heat must be produced to replace that which is lost. BMR also depends on gender. It is greater for males than females. And, as we grow older, our BMR decreases. BMR depends, too, on the amount of thyroid hormone the body produces and on body temperature. A fever of one degree Celsius (1.8 degrees Fahrenheit) increases the BMR by about 13 percent. People who secrete more than normal amounts of thyroid hormone have higher metabolic rates. Those who secrete less than normal amounts of thyroid hormone have lower metabolic rates. Finally, emotions and drugs, such as caffeine, can increase an individual's metabolic rate.

Generally, a person's BMR can be closely approximated from age, gender, and surface area. Table 1 shows how basal metabolism per square meter (m²) of body area is related to gender and age. The graph in Figure 10 provides a way to find one's surface area from his height and weight. By using the table and the graph you can find the expected BMR for any individual.

Suppose a 13-year-old boy weighs 110 pounds and is 5 feet 3 inches tall. What can we expect his BMR to be? From Table 1, we see that a 13-year-old boy, on the average, burns 50 Calories every hour for each square meter of body area. To find the boy's body

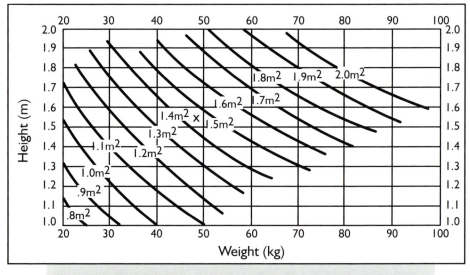

Figure 10. To determine a person's surface area, find her weight on the horizontal axis. Then go up that vertical weight line to the horizontal line that represents her height. The intersection of these two lines, on or near the curved lines showing area, will give her surface area. For example, say a person weighs 48 kg and is 1.55 m tall. His weight and height lines meet at a point shown as an "X" on the graph. Since this point is about midway between the curves representing 1.4 m² and 1.5 m², we estimate his surface area to be 1.45 m².

area, we look at Figure 10. The graph uses meters to measure height and kilograms for weight. So we must first change inches (in) to meters (m) and pounds (lb) to kilograms (kg). Since 39.37 in = 1.0 m and 2.2 lb = 1.0 kg, therefore:

63 in ÷ 39.37 in/m = 1.6 m and 110 lb ÷ 2.2 lb/kg = 50 kg

The graph shows us that a person who weighs 50 kg and is 1.6 m tall has a surface area of almost 1.5 square meters (m^2). His BMR, therefore, is approximately:

1.5 m^2 x 50 Cal/h/m^2 = 75 Cal/h or 1800 Cal/day

The value calculated in this example is an average for the person described. However, smaller factors, such as the amount of thyroid hormone secreted, body temperature, caffeine, and emotions, can affect an individual's BMR.

Use Table 1 and Figure 10 to calculate your BMR. What is the BMR of each of your volunteers? Do you suspect that any of these people have a BMR that is actually higher than the one you calculated? If so, what makes you think so? Do you suspect that any of them have a BMR that is lower than the one you calculated?

Table 1: Average Basal Metabolism for Males and Females*

Age (years)	Calories per hour for each square meter of body area (Cal/h/m^2)	
	Male	Female
2–12	52	50
12–14	50	46
14–16	46	43
16–18	43	40
18–20	41	38
20–40	40	37
40–60	38	36

*Adapted from Table 26-5 of *Anthony's Textbook of Anatomy & Physiology*, Thibodeau, Gary A., and Kevin T. Patton, Mosby-Year Book, Inc., 1994.

5-2
Total Metabolic Rate

Total metabolic rate is the energy required by the body per unit of time. It is usually expressed as Calories per hour or Calories per day. It includes the BMR, which is often more

than half of the total metabolic rate, as well as the energy needed for muscles to carry out all the activities we do each day. It involves, too, the effect of food on metabolism. After we eat, our metabolic rate increases because energy is required to metabolize the food. Carbohydrates and fats raise the metabolic rate by about 5 percent; proteins increase the rate by about 30 percent. Table 3 provides information that can be used to estimate the total metabolic rate and the energy needed for an entire day's activity.

Consider an active 50-kg boy who sleeps for 10 hours, studies for 3 hours, sits in classes for 4 hours, watches television for 1 hour, spends an hour walking to and from school, plays baseball for 2 hours, rides his bike for an hour to travel 10 miles, does yard work for 1 hour, and reads in a chair for an hour. A summary of the boy's activities and energy requirements is listed in Table 2.

Table 2: Boy's Activities and Energy Requirements

Activity	Energy Required (Hours x energy in Cal/kg per hour x body weight = Cal)
sleep	10 x 0.80 x 50 = 400
study	3 x 2.5 x 50 = 375
sit in class	4 x 1.3 x 50 = 260
sit for TV	1 x 0.9 x 50 = 45
walking	1 x 4.4 x 50 = 220
baseball	2 x 4.6 x 50 = 460
biking	1 x 7.0 x 50 = 350
yard work	1 x 3.1 x 50 = 155
reading	1 x 2.0 x 50 = 100
	24 hr 2,365 Cal

Table 3: Energy Required to Perform Various Activities

Activity	Average energy per kilogram of weight (Cal/kg) to carry on the activity for one hour
baseball	4.6
basketball	6.2
bicycling (10 mph)	7.0
dancing	4.4
eating	1.3
football	7.5
golf	4.8
housework	3.5
jogging	5.5
judo, wrestling, karate	11.0
office work	2.6
reading	2.0
reclining	0.9
running	11.0
skating	9.0
skiing	8.4
soccer	7.8
sleeping	0.8
swimming	6.3
sitting at rest	2.0
sitting in class	1.3
studying	2.5
standing	1.3
tennis	8.2
walking	4.4
watching television	0.9
yard work	3.1

Keep a record of your own activities for an average day. Then use Table 3 to estimate your energy requirements for that day. How do they compare with those given in Table 4? Were you more or less active than the average person your age?

Table 4: Average Daily Energy Requirements for People of Different Ages and Gender

Person	Energy needed for one day (Cal)
Infant: 2–9 months	1,000
Child: 8 years old	2,100
Boy: 15 years old	3,000
Girl: 15 years old	2,500
Woman: inactive	1,900
Woman: active	2,200
Man: inactive	2,500
Man: active	3,000

Ask a few volunteers to keep records of their daily activities. Then show them how to calculate their energy requirements.

5-3
Meeting Energy Requirements

The energy you need to carry out your activities, such as those you recorded in Experiment 5-2, comes from the food you eat. For example, a slice of white

Things you will need:

• cookbook
• Figure 11
• results of Experiment 5-2

bread will provide 70 Calories of energy when it is metabolized in your body. The energy available from servings of various foods can be found in most cookbooks. But foods provide more than energy. They also contain vitamins and minerals that are essential for good health and chemicals that are used to build new tissue and complex substances needed for life.

The food pyramid, such as the one seen in Figure 11, clarifies the kinds of food you need to maintain good health. It is also important to remember that fats should make up no more than 30 percent of your diet, that about 12 percent of your food should be proteins, and that the rest should be carbohydrates.

Do some research on food values, and, considering your own energy use, design a diet that meets all your nutritional needs.

Carbohydrate Loading

Carbohydrates are found in such foods as pasta, fruits, vegetables, and grains. The digestion of complex carbohydrates, such as the starch in pasta, begins in the mouth and continues in the stomach and small intestine. The end product of this digestive process is glucose, a soluble sugar that is absorbed by the blood and carried to the cells of the body. Excess glucose is converted to glycogen, an insoluble starch that is stored in muscles and the liver.

During exercise, glucose is "burned" in the body to provide energy. As the concentration of glucose in the blood decreases, the pancreas secretes glucagon. Glucagon causes cells in the liver to convert glycogen to glucose, which tends to raise the amount of glucose in the blood and provide the "fuel" needed for muscular action.

Food Pyramid

Fats, Oils, and Sweets
Minimal servings

Milk, Yogurt, &
Cheese
2–3
servings
daily
4 for children

Meat, Fish, Poultry,
Dry Beans, Nuts,
Seeds, and Eggs
2–3
servings
daily

Vegetables
3–5
servings
daily

Fruits
2–4
servings
daily

Bread, Cereal, Rice, and Pasta Group
6–11 servings daily

Figure 11. The food pyramid indicates the types of food and number of daily servings that should make up the human diet.

Some athletes who participate in endurance sports (events that take two or more hours of steady exercise), such as distance running, eat large amounts of carbohydrates prior to competition, a practice known as carbohydrate loading. Some will simply eat a dinner of pasta, potatoes, rice, and bread, along with fruits and vegetables, the night before the athletic event. Others believe it is best to remove most of the body's glycogen before loading the body with carbohydrates. These athletes exercise vigorously about six days before the competition to reduce their body's glycogen supply. They then eat a high-protein, low-carbohydrate diet for three days to keep their glycogen level low. The theory is that starving the liver and muscle cells of glycogen for several days will stimulate them to store excess amounts of glycogen. For three days before the event, they provide the excess glycogen by eating foods rich in carbohydrates.

5-4*
The Pinch Test

Most athletes have bodies that are less than 20 percent fat. Most of their weight is lean weight—muscle, not fat. To build and maintain muscle cells you have to exercise. Everyone who is healthy should exercise at least 30 minutes each day. Even a daily walk at 3–4 miles per hour for half an hour each day will help, but an hour or more of vigorous exercise is better.

Things you will need:

• ruler

• a few volunteers

One way to determine if a person is too fat is the pinch test. The flesh on the back of a person's arm as it hangs by his side is squeezed between a tester's thumb and fingers. If the pinched flesh is an inch or more thick, the person is probably overweight.

Do you pass the pinch test? Do your volunteers pass the pinch test? **Be sure to explain the test and ask their permission before you test them.**

If you are overweight, you need to consume food with less energy than your daily activities require. In that way, some of the fat stored in your body will be used for energy. Whether you are overweight or not, design a diet that provides less energy than your daily activities require. Bear in mind that such a diet should contain all the essential vitamins and minerals you need. **Check with a doctor or nutritionist before you go on any diet.**

Exploring on Your Own

A better indicator of whether a person is overweight is his or her lean body weight (LBW). How is a person's LBW determined?

Girls and women normally have a higher percentage of body fat than do boys and men. Does more body fat per pound provide some advantage for the female gender? Hint: Men are generally larger than women.

Stand on a spring-type bathroom scale. Suddenly bend your knees to lower your weight. What appears to happen to your weight? Why do you think it happens?

6

Muscles and Exercise

To play sports, or do anything for that matter, we move by using our muscles. The major muscles found in the human body are shown in Figure 12.

In this chapter you will learn about some of the properties of muscles and see how they work and why they sometimes don't work as we would like them to. You will begin this chapter by dissecting a chicken wing. By doing so, you will see what muscles look like and how they connect to bones.

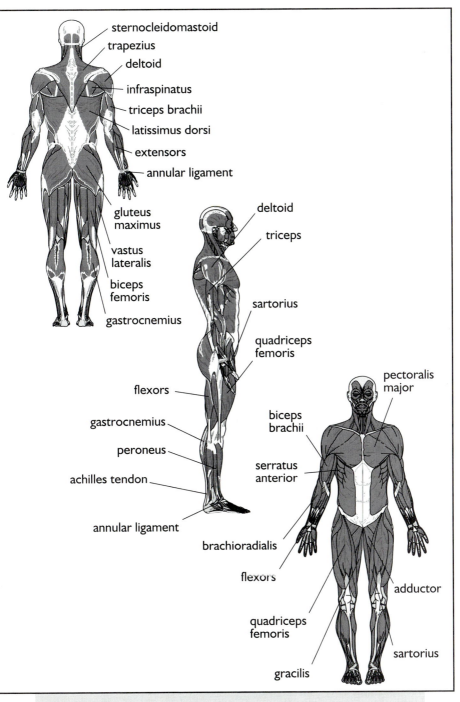

Figure 12. The major muscles of the body are shown from the back, side, and front.

6-1*
Muscles in a Chicken's Wing

Obtain an uncooked chicken wing from a meat market. Place the wing on some newspaper, and **ask an adult to help you cut it apart.** You will need a sharp knife, a pair of tweezers, scissors, and a probe. Most of the skin can be pulled away with your fingers. As you pull away the skin, notice the connective tissue that connects it to the muscles beneath it.

Notice that each muscle is covered by a very thin transparent membrane. With tweezers and a probe (a stick or finishing nail can serve as a probe), separate the muscles from one another. See if you can find where each muscle attaches to a bone. The muscles are attached to bones by tough, white, fibrous tendons. Pull on each muscle to see how its contraction makes a bone move.

Things you will need:
- chicken wing
- newspapers
- an adult
- sharp knife
- tweezers
- scissors
- probe, such as a slender stick or finishing nail
- paper towels
- garbage container
- soap and water

Using scissors cut the tendons and remove the muscles so you can see the bones. As Figure 13 shows, the major bones in a chicken wing are very similar to your arm bones. Can you find the humerus? The radius? The ulna? How do the carpals, metacarpals, and phalanges of a chicken's "arm" differ from yours?

Now that you have exposed the bones, find the wide, tough, white ligaments that connect the humerus to the radius and ulna. Cut away the ligaments with scissors in order to see the ends of the bones. Notice the shiny cartilage that covers the ends of the bones. How does the cartilage protect the bones? Do you find anything else within the joint (the space between the bones)?

56

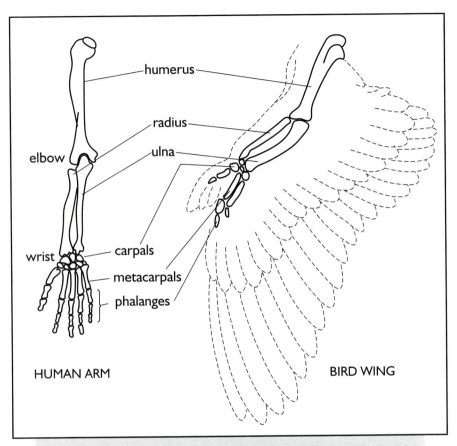

humerus

radius

elbow

ulna

wrist

carpals

metacarpals

phalanges

HUMAN ARM

BIRD WING

Figure 13. The bones of the human arm are very similar to the bones of a bird's wing.

When you have finished, place all the chicken wing tissues in the garbage and then **wash your hands and utensils thoroughly with soap and water.**

Exploring on Your Own

One of the most serious athletic injuries involves tearing the anterior cruciate ligament in the knee. Investigate this injury and try to explain why it is so much more common among women than men.

6-2*
Muscles Are Levers

Archimedes, an early Greek scientist, is believed to have said, "Give me a place to stand and I will move the earth." His experiments with levers led Archimedes to discover that a

small force applied at a large distance from the fulcrum (the point about which a lever turns) will move a heavy object close to the fulcrum. Figure 14 shows a simple lever and the names of the forces and distances that are used in describing this simple machine.

The effort arm is the distance from the fulcrum to the point where Archimedes would have applied a force (the effort force) if he had a place to stand. The resistance arm is the distance from the fulcrum to the resistance force, or load, that opposes the effort force. In Archimedes' example, the earth's weight would be the resistance force.

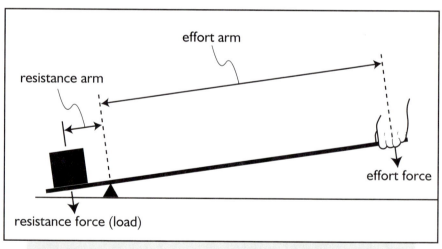

Figure 14. The lever, shown here, is a simple machine. Together, muscles and bones form levers in our bodies.

Levers are classified as one of three types, depending on the positions of the fulcrum, effort force, and resistance force. First-class levers (Figures 14 and 15a), such as a crowbar, have the fulcrum between the two forces. If the effort arm is much longer than the resistance arm, a small effort force can move a large load (weight), or resistance force.

With second-class levers (Figure 15b), such as a wheelbarrow, the resistance force is applied at a point between the fulcrum and the effort force. As a result, the distance through which the effort force moves is always greater than the distance the load is moved.

In third-class levers (Figure 15c), such as a fishing pole, the effort force is between the fulcrum and the load. For all third-class levers, the effort force must be greater than the resistance force if

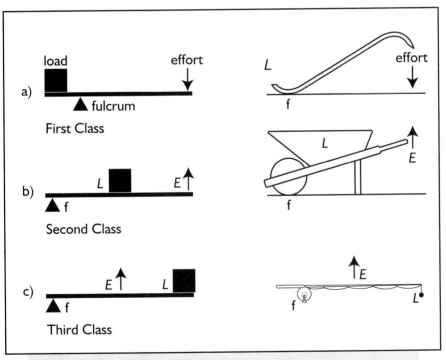

Figure 15. These drawings show first-, second-, and third-class levers, as well as examples of each class.

the resistance force (load) is to move. The advantage of a third-class lever is that moving the effort force a small distance can produce a large movement of the load, or weight, as any fisherman will tell you.

To obtain a firsthand look and feel for first-class levers place a pencil under a rigid wooden ruler. The pencil will serve as a fulcrum. Put a book on one end of the ruler and place the pencil under the center of the ruler, as shown in Figure 16a. Let the book's weight push down on the end of the ruler. Use your hand only to prevent the book from falling over. Press on the other end of the ruler with your finger to lift the book. Next, move the pencil (fulcrum) to a point close to the book (Figure 16b). Lift the book again by pressing down on the end of the ruler opposite the book. Finally, place the fulcrum near the end of the ruler opposite the book (Figure 16c). Once again lift the book by pushing down with your finger on the opposite end of the ruler.

In which case was it easiest to lift the book? In which case was it hardest? How does the ratio of the effort arm to the resistance arm affect the size of the effort force needed to lift the same object?

Design experiments of your own to obtain a firsthand look and feel for second- and third-class levers.

There are many muscles and bones that act as levers in your body. One end of a muscle that applies an effort force has its origin (attachment) on a bone that does not move. The muscle's insertion (attachment of its other end) is to the bone (lever) that moves. It is this bone that moves against the resistance force.

To examine a muscle-bone lever, hold your arm out straight and place a weight in your upturned palm. Place the fingers of your other hand on the inside of the elbow joint of the arm that holds the weight. You can feel the tendons of the brachialis and biceps muscles that attach to the lower arm as you bend your arm and lift the weight. Figure 17 shows how this body lever works. Where is the fulcrum for this body lever? Is this a first-, second-, or third-class

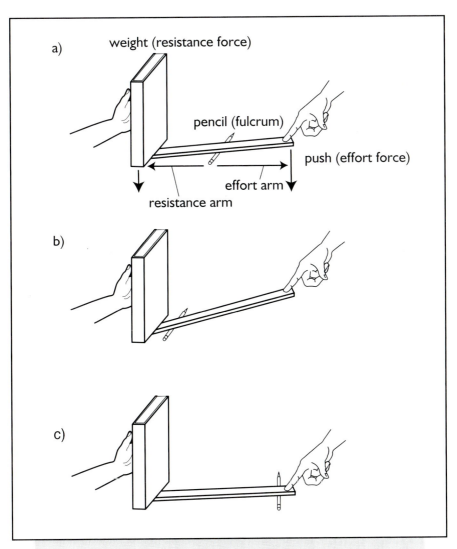

a) weight (resistance force)

pencil (fulcrum)

push (effort force)

resistance arm

effort arm

b)

c)

Figure 16. Simple experiments with a first-class lever.

lever? How will the effort force exerted by the muscle compare with the weight held in the hand?

Put your chin on your chest and your hand on the back of your neck. As you lift and tilt your head backward, you can feel the splenius capitis muscles (see Figure 18a), inserted on both sides of the occipital bone at the back of your skull, contracting to pull your head up and backward as it turns on the atlas. (The atlas is the first, or top, vertebra of the backbone.) The weight of your head can be considered to be at the center of your skull. Which class of lever is this muscle-bone lever?

The opposing muscle (Figure 18b), which pulls your head downward, is the sternocleidomastoid. Can you feel its tendon on your clavicle (collar bone) when you pull your chin down onto your chest?

Consider the act of throwing a ball. What muscles are involved? Which are opposing muscles? What muscle-bone levers does the action require?

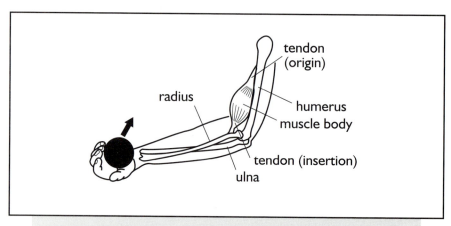

Figure 17. Your upper arm muscle and lower arm bone act as a lever.

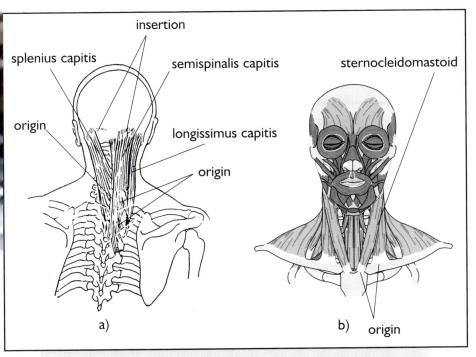

insertion

splenius capitis

semispinalis capitis

sternocleidomastoid

origin

longissimus capitis

origin

a)

b) origin

Figure 18. a) Contraction of the splenius capitis, semispinalis capitis, and longissimus capitis muscles pulls the skull back. b) Contraction of the sternocleidomastoid muscle pulls the head onto the chest.

Exploring on Your Own

Using a book on anatomy that shows how muscles connect to bones, find examples of levers in the human body. Classify each of these levers as first-, second-, or third-class levers.

6-3*
Muscle Pairs

If a bone can be moved to a certain position, it can be returned to its previous setting. Muscles are paired so movements can be reversed. You can flex (bend) your arm by con-

Things you will need:
• spring-type bathroom scale
• chair
• wall
• a partner

tracting your biceps and/or brachialis muscles. The triceps brachii extends (straightens) the arm. What do you know about this muscle just from its name?

When your arm is flexed, place your hand on the back of your upper arm. Do you feel the triceps contract as you fully straighten your arm? What can you assume about the location of the triceps' insertion? Where might its origin(s) be located?

Muscles can only contract and pull on a bone; they cannot expand and push a bone. Consequently, one muscle, or set of muscles, such as the biceps and brachialis, bends (flexes) a joint. Another muscle, such as the triceps, straightens (extends) the joint. Muscles that bend a joint are called flexors; muscles that straighten a joint are called extensors.

In some paired muscles, one muscle or muscle group is stronger than the other. With a spring-type bathroom scale you can compare the strengths of muscle pairs. Consider the muscles that allow you to kick both forward and backward. Are they of equal strength?

To find out, stand facing a wall. Place the scale upright against the wall as shown in Figure 19. (If necessary, adjust the zero position of the scale.) Have a partner read the scale as you push your toes forward against the scale. With what force can you push your foot forward? Which muscles are you using? (See Figure 12.) Now turn around and push your heel backward against the scale. Again, have a partner read the scale. With what force can you push your foot backward? Which muscles are you using now?

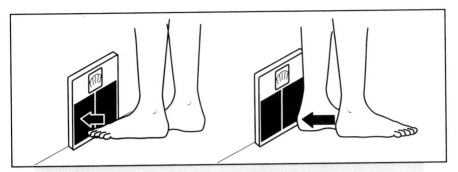

Figure 19. How does the strength of the muscles that push your foot forward compare with the strength of the muscles that push your foot backward?

How does the relative strength of the muscle pairs used to push your foot forward and backward compare with that of your partner?

Next, place the scale so you can compare the strength of the flexor muscles that bend your arm with the strength of the extensor muscle that straightens your arm. How do the strengths of the flexor and extensor muscles compare? Are they equal or unequal in strength? How does the strength of these same muscles in your partner compare?

Compare the strengths of the muscle pairs used to turn your toes upward or downward. Which muscles are used to make these movements?

Compare the strengths of the muscle pairs used to flex your fingers toward your palm or extend them away from your palm. Which muscles are used to make these movements?

Compare the strengths of the muscle pairs used to move your head forward or to move it backward. Which muscles are used to make these movements?

Compare the strengths of the muscle pairs used to flex or extend your leg at the knee. Which muscles are used to make these movements?

Exploring on Your Own

Through training, can you increase the strength of the weaker member of a muscle pair?

6-4*
Muscles and Muscle Use

Muscles are attached to bones by tendons. One end of a muscle, its origin, is generally attached to a bone that remains fixed. The other end of the muscle, its insertion, is attached to a bone that moves when the muscle contracts. Figure 20a shows the origin and insertion of the brachialis muscle, which lies under your biceps brachii and is

Things you will need:

- photographs of various athletes, such as swimmers, runners, and gymnasts

- tape measure

- horizontal bar (a tree limb will do)

- a partner

- gymnasium with weight lifting equipment (optional) and adult supervisor

used to bend your arm at the elbow. As the drawing reveals, the origin of the brachialis lies on the humerus (upper arm bone). Its insertion is on the ulna (one of the two bones of the lower arm).

Extend your arm with your palm downward. Now, bend your arm. When you do this, the brachialis contracts, pulling the ulna bone upward. If you then turn your palm toward your face and bend your arm, you will feel the biceps brachii bulge as it contracts. As Figure 20b shows, the insertion of biceps brachii is on the radius (the other lower arm bone). Its two origins are on the bones of the shoulder.

To straighten your arm, the triceps brachii (Figure 20c) on the back of your upper arm (humerus) contracts. You can feel the triceps bulge as it contracts by placing your hand on the back of your upper arm as you straighten that arm.

Identify and feel other muscles as they contract. Which muscles allow you to bend your fingers to your palm? Which muscles enable you to extend your fingers? Can you see the tendons under your skin as you contract these two sets of muscles?

What happens when you contract the quadriceps muscles in your thigh? What happens when you contract the gastrocnemius

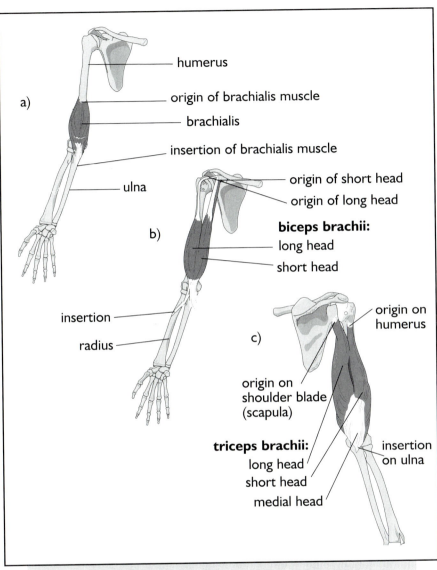

a) humerus

origin of brachialis muscle

brachialis

insertion of brachialis muscle

ulna

origin of short head

origin of long head

biceps brachii:
long head
short head

b)

insertion

radius

c)

origin on humerus

origin on shoulder blade (scapula)

triceps brachii:
long head
short head
medial head

insertion on ulna

Figure 20. a) The origin and insertion of the brachialis muscle that lies on the upper arm bone (humerus). b) The origin and insertion of the biceps brachii. The "bi" part of biceps indicates that the muscle has two parts. c) The origin and insertion of the triceps brachii. As you might guess, the "tri" part of this muscle's name indicates that it has three parts. Its origins are on the scapula (shoulder blade) and the back of the humerus. Its insertion is on the elbow end of the ulna.

(calf) muscle? What muscles are paired with the gastrocnemius and quadriceps? (See Figure 12a.)

Think about the muscles most used in such sports as swimming, hockey, tennis, and track. Predict the muscles that would be most developed in athletes who participate in these sports. Then look at photographs or, if possible, people who engage in these sports at a competitive level. How does their muscle development compare with your predictions?

Making Muscles Grow

If muscles are not used, they atrophy (decrease in size). However, if they are used to their fullest strength, they will grow, because muscle cells enlarge or increase in number. To see that this is true, use a tape measure to find the circumference of your right and left biceps muscles when flexed. Is one biceps bigger than the other? If it is, can you explain why? Then, after stretching and warming up, find a horizontal bar (a tree limb will do) that is just above your reach. When you grasp it with both hands and hang from it, your elbows should be straight and your feet just off the ground. Slowly raise your body until your chin is just above the bar (Figure 21). Pause for a moment, slowly lower your body back to your starting position, then lift your body again. Repeat this process of doing chin-ups several times a day. When you can raise your body a dozen times easily, have a partner apply some resistance by holding onto your waist or legs. As you gain strength in your biceps over weeks and months, have your partner increase the resistance.

Every week remeasure the circumference of both your biceps. What evidence do you have that your biceps muscles have grown? Does one biceps grow faster than the other? If it does, can you explain why?

If you have access to a gymnasium with weight lifting equipment, you can, **under adult supervision**, do similar experiments to strengthen other muscles such as your quadriceps and hamstrings,

Figure 21. Chin-ups will strengthen your biceps.

the opposing muscles that flex and extend your legs. How much will these muscles grow when used to lift weights? Which muscle, quadriceps or hamstrings, is stronger when you begin your experiment? What is the strength ratio of these two muscles? Which muscle is stronger after several months? Has the strength ratio changed?

Exploring on Your Own

Do some research to find the strongest muscle in the human body. What muscle is it? Design and carry out an experiment to determine how strong it is.

Muscle Force and Angle

Does the maximum effort force (pull) that a muscle can exert on a body lever (bone) depend on the angle at which it pulls on that bone?

Things you will need:

- a partner
- spring-type bathroom scale
- table
- chair
- notebook and pen or pencil

To find out, you can measure the force that your brachialis and biceps brachii muscles exert at different angles when you bend your arm at the elbow. To do this, have a partner support a spring-type bathroom scale against the underside of a table. The number on the scale should read zero and be visible to your partner, who will record the data in this experiment. Sit in a chair beside the scale. With your arm fully extended, the angle between these

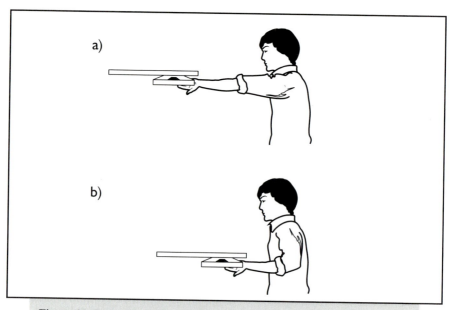

Figure 22. Does the angle at which a muscle pulls on a bone affect the force that the muscle can exert on the bone? In (a), the muscle acts at an angle of 180 degrees. In (b), the muscle acts at an angle of 90 degrees.

upper arm muscles and the lower bones of your arm where their insertions lie is approximately 180 degrees (Figure 22a). What force can your upturned palm exert on the bathroom scale at this angle?

Repeat the experiment with your arm bent at a right angle (Figure 22b) so that the angle between these muscles and your lower arm bones is approximately 90 degrees. What force can you exert on the scale now?

Repeat the experiment with your arm at angles of approximately 45, 120, 135, and 150 degrees. What do you find?

Repeat the experiment to find the force that your triceps muscle can exert on the lower arm at different angles. The triceps muscle, shown in Figure 20c, is used to straighten your arm.

From the data you have obtained, what can you conclude about the relationship between the effort force (pull) that a muscle can exert on a bone and the angle between the long axis of the bone and the muscle?

6-6*
Measuring Your Reaction Time

Success in athletics depends to a large extent on quickness, on the ability to respond rapidly to a stimulus such as an approaching ball or opponent. In this experiment you will find out how quickly you can react to a visual stimulus. You will see something start to move. A nerve impulse from your eye will travel to the occipital (rear) region of your brain. From there, another impulse will travel to a center in your brain that will, in turn, send impulses to the muscles of your forearm. You will react by using the muscles in your forearm to bring your thumb and fingers together.

Things you will need:

• desk or table
• 1-foot ruler
• Table 5
• pen or pencil
• notebook
• several volunteers of different gender and ages
• tape measure

To do the experiment, rest the heel of your dominant hand on the edge of a desk or table. Your thumb and fingers should be about an inch apart. Your friend is to hold a ruler, which he will drop. He holds it so that the zero end of the ruler is even with your thumb and index finger.

Watch the bottom of the ruler. When your friend releases the ruler and you see the end of the ruler begin to fall, bring your thumb and fingers together. How far did the ruler fall before you caught it? You can tell how far it fell by seeing what inch-line on the ruler lies under your thumb or index finger. The faster you react, the shorter the distance the ruler will fall.

Record the distance the ruler fell. Then repeat the experiment four more times. For each trial, record the distance the ruler fell. Then calculate the average distance the ruler fell. Use Table 5 to determine your reaction time.

Table 5: Reaction Times for Various Distances Ruler Falls Before Being Caught

Distance ruler fell (inches)	Reaction time (seconds)
1	0.072
2	0.102
3	0.125
4	0.144
5	0.161
6	0.177
7	0.191
8	0.204
9	0.216
10	0.228
11	0.239
12	0.250

Suppose you catch the ruler at 6¾ inches. How can you estimate your reaction time?

Repeat the experiment using your other hand. Does your dominant hand react faster than your other hand?

Repeat the experiment with several volunteers. Choose people of different gender and ages. Measure their reaction times for each of their hands. Does hand dominance affect reaction time? Do girls react faster than boys? Does age affect reaction time?

Your reaction time is related to the time it takes for a visual nerve stimulus to move from your eye to your brain and for another nerve stimulus to travel from your brain to the muscles in your forearm. Using a tape measure and the data you have collected, make an estimate of the speed at which nerve impulses travel along nerve fibers.

Exploring on Your Own

Measure your reaction time at different times of the day, such as just after you get up, just before lunch, late afternoon, and just before you go to bed. Does time of day affect your reaction time? If it does, can you explain why?

Explain how the reaction times for different distances of fall in Table 5 were determined.

6-7*
Tired Muscles

When the same muscle is used over and over again, it tires. The energy needed to make a muscle contract comes from chemical changes that occur in the muscle cells. One of the products of these reactions is lactic acid.

Things you will need:

• 2 partners

• watch or clock with second hand

• notebook and pen or pencil

• graph paper

Muscle fatigue is caused by the accumulation of lactic acid in the muscle cells. In aerobic exercise, the lactic acid is removed by the blood so that it does not accumulate, but anaerobic exercise of a muscle leads to its fatigue.

About 20 percent of the lactic acid eventually reacts with oxygen to produce carbon dioxide and water with the release of energy. The rest of the lactic acid is changed to glycogen, a starch that serves to store energy. Glycogen is readily changed to glucose sugar, which is a main energy source for the human body.

To see the effects of repeated use of muscles, stand with your right arm raised to shoulder height with your palm turned downward. Have a partner with a watch or clock act as timer. When you hear the timer say, "Go," begin closing and opening your right hand to make as many fists as possible during a twenty-second period. Another partner will count the number of fists you make during the twenty-second interval. At the end of twenty seconds the timer will say, "Stop!" At that point, you will drop your arm and rest for twenty seconds. The person who did the counting will record the number of fists you made during this first trial in a data table similar to the one shown in Table 6.

After resting for twenty seconds, you will repeat the experiment with the same hand. Continue to do this until you have completed five trials with twenty seconds of rest between each trial. Then repeat the experiment with your left hand.

Table 6: Data table for Measuring Muscle Fatigue

	Number of fists made				
Subject's name	Trial 1	Trial 2	Trial 3	Trial 4	Trial 5

After you have completed your trials with both hands, have the timer serve as the subject, while you count and the counter becomes the timer. Repeat the entire experiment three times so that all three members of the team serve as a subject.

Plot a graph of the number of fists you made in 20 seconds versus the number of the trial. Plot the data for both hands on the same graph. Have each subject plot his or her own data on a separate graph. How can you explain the results as depicted on the graphs? Are the results for both hands the same? If not, can you explain why?

Since lactic acid reacts with oxygen, you might expect that increasing the concentration of oxygen in the body would reduce lactic acid levels and help to prevent muscle fatigue. After an hour or more of rest, you can test this hypothesis. Simply repeat the experiment, but during all five trials and during the rest periods between trials, have the subject breathe deeply. That is, he or she should take in more air than usual with each breath. This will bring more air (and oxygen) into contact with the blood and thus provide more oxygen to the muscles.

Have all three subjects repeat the experiment. Record and graph the data for each subject. Do the experimental results tend to confirm or deny the hypothesis? Explain why you think so.

Exploring on Your Own

Repeat Experiment 6-7 with your arms at your sides rather than raised. Are the results the same? If they are not, explain why they are different.

Investigate where and how glycogen is stored in the body.

What is meant by "oxygen debt"? How is oxygen debt related to Experiment 6-7?

Investigate the role of ATP (adenosine triphosphate) in muscle contraction.

6-8
The Well Balanced Athlete

A team member who is constantly falling to the field or floor is not helping his or her teammates. A good athlete must have good balance. A number of factors are involved in maintaining one's balance. At the rear of the brain, under the cerebrum,

Things you will need:
- notebook and pen or pencil
- several volunteers
- clock or watch with second hand
- swivel chair with arms
- an adult

lies the cerebellum, as shown in Figure 23. Nerve impulses passing through the cerebellum coordinate and control muscle contractions including those that keep your body balanced.

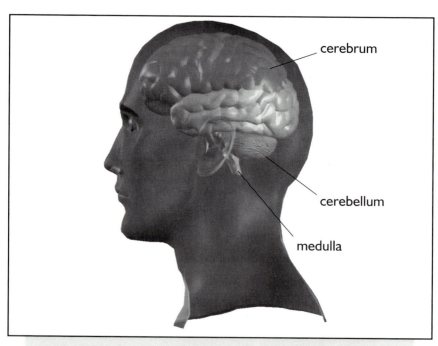

cerebrum

cerebellum

medulla

Figure 23. The three main parts of the brain are the cerebrum, cerebellum, and medulla. The cerebellum, which enables us to maintain our balance, lies under the cerebrum. The medulla connects the brain and spinal cord.

The inner ear fills a hollowed-out portion of the skull. Within the inner ear are three semicircular canals, shown in Figure 24. These appropriately named tubes lie at right angles to one another and are filled with fluid and nerve endings. Movements of the head, which may or may not be accompanied by body movements, cause fluid in one or more of the canals to move and bend hair cells, sending nerve impulses to the cerebellum.

The cerebellum also receives nerve impulses from muscles, joints, the brain, and the spinal cord. It sends impulses to the muscles, other parts of the brain, including the rear part of the cerebrum where light is perceived, and to various levels of the spinal cord where impulses are sent to muscle cells. Although we are not aware of it, the cerebellum enables the body to maintain balance and

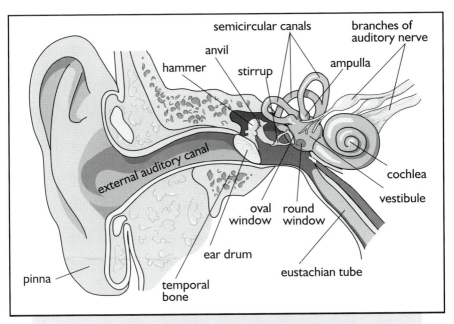

Figure 24. A view of the human ear showing the outer ear, which extends to the ear drum; the middle ear, which contains three small bones (hammer, anvil, and stirrup), and the inner ear where the semicircular canals and cochlea are located.

respond to changes in position. Damage to the cerebellum results in weakness and loss of muscle control so severe that a victim may be unable to walk or talk.

In this experiment you will test subjects' ability to maintain their balance under four different conditions. Record the data for each subject in a table like Table 7.

Ask a subject to try to stand on one foot (either foot) for 30 seconds with eyes open. A subject may move his or her arms, but must remain on one foot. Record the time the subject is able to maintain balance on one foot. A few may be able to stand for the entire 30-second period.

After a 30-second rest period, ask the subject to repeat the experiment with his or her eyes firmly shut. Again, record the time the subject is able to remain balanced.

For the third trial, following a 30-second rest period, have the subject sit in a swivel chair that has arms. **Ask an adult** to turn the chair around six times while the subject is seated in the chair with eyes open. The adult should turn the chair rapidly but not so swiftly that the subject has trouble remaining seated.

Immediately after the sixth spin, ask the subject to stand on one foot with eyes open for 30 seconds. Record the time the subject is

Table 7: Maintaining Balance Under Different Conditions

| | Time (in seconds) balance maintained while standing | | | |
Subject's name	Eyes open	Eyes closed	After turning (eyes open)	After turning (eyes closed)

able to remain balanced. **The adult should stand beside the subject to provide support should he begin to fall.**

Finally, after another rest period, **ask an adult** to again spin the subject and stand by. This time the subject is to keep eyes closed while spinning and while standing. Again, record the time he or she is able to remain balanced on one foot.

Repeat the entire experiment on as many people as possible. Does the ability to maintain one's balance appear to be related to athletic ability? Does it appear to be related to age, gender, weight, or height?

On the basis of your data, does vision play an important role in maintaining balance? What evidence do you have to support your conclusion?

Under which conditions are the semicircular canals most affected in this experiment?

Does rotation affect a person's ability to maintain his or her balance? If it does, why do you think it does?

7

Exercise and Conditioning

People who are in good physical condition are able to exercise vigorously because their hearts and other muscles are strong and durable, they have plenty of red blood cells, they use the air they breathe efficiently, and their bodies contain little fat tissue.

An excellent way to test your physical fitness is to participate in the President's Physical Fitness Challenge. Many schools across the nation participate in this challenge each year. You can ask your physical education teacher about this test if your school does not already participate in the program. You can access the program on your computer at www.indiana.edu/~preschal.

Another way to determine whether or not people are in good physical condition is to have them do the tests of physical condition described in Experiment 7-1.

7-1
Tests of Physical Condition

Here are some tests that can be used to determine physical condition. Please do not try any of these tests if you or others involved have not been participating in some type of physical activity over the last few weeks. Instead, begin some type of exercise program, such as walking, swimming, or jogging, and then use the tests to monitor your progress.

Things you will need:
- clock or watch with a second hand
- notebook and pen or pencil
- yardstick or measuring tape
- spring-type bathroom scale
- a bench 12, 14, 16, 18, or 20 inches high, depending on your height

Before doing any of these tests, be sure you warm up and stretch your muscles to prevent any injury, as described in Chapter 2. Be sure to cool down afterward.

Ability Tests

Balance:
- Stand on your toes with your heels together, arms extended out in front of your body, with eyes closed for 20 seconds or longer.
- Stand on one foot with the other foot straight out in front of you. Hold your arms out front at shoulder height. Rise onto the ball of the foot you are standing on and hold for ten seconds.

Flexibility:
- Sit on the floor with your feet against a wall. Keep the feet together and the legs straight. Bend forward at the hips. Reach for the wall with closed fists. You should be able to touch the wall with your closed fists.

- Stand with your legs together and straight. You should be able to touch your fingers to the floor.

Arm strength:
- Lie face down on the floor. Place your hands under your shoulders. The elbows should stay close to the body. Keeping the legs and body straight, press off the floor until the arms are fully extended and the body is completely off the floor. Girls should be able to do this once. Boys should be able to do it three times.

Upper body strength:
- Boys should be able to do 8–10 push-ups with hands at shoulder level and away from the body.
- Girls should be able to do 6–8 push-ups.

Muscular endurance and strength:
- Lie on your side on the floor. Lift your top leg up until your feet are 2 to 3 ft apart. You should be able to do 10 lifts with each leg.

Leg power:
- Stand with legs together and toes just behind a line. Bend your knees and jump forward. You should be able to jump a horizontal distance equal to your height.

Hand strength:
- Hold a spring-type bathroom scale, one hand on each side, thumbs above and fingers beneath. Squeeze the scale as hard as you can. Table 8 gives a rough estimate of your hand strength.

Table 8: An Evaluation of Hand Strength

Strength Rating	Pounds read on scale	
	Adolescent boys	Adolescent girls
Excellent	150 or more	80 or more
Good	120–150	60–80
Fair	90–120	40–60
Poor	Less than 90	Less than 40

Muscular endurance:

- Lie on your back. Put your hands behind your head with the elbows out to the side. Have someone hold your feet on the floor with your knees bent and your feet a little over a foot from your buttocks. Raise your upper body so the elbow touches the opposite knee, right elbow to left knee, then left elbow to right knee. Count each touch. Make sure your elbows return to the ground after each knee touch. See how many you can do in one minute. Table 9 gives a rough estimate of muscular endurance.

Table 9: An Evaluation of Muscular Endurance

Muscular endurance	Number of elbow to knee touches in 1 minute	
	Adolescent boys	Adolescent girls
Excellent	over 35	over 45
Good	30–35	35–45
Average	20–30	20–35
Fair	15–20	10–20
Poor	10–15	0–10

Endurance of vigorous exercise:

- Run in place for 1 minute, lifting your feet up at least four inches. If, after one minute, you feel out of breath and have a pulse of more than 100 beats a minute, you do not have good endurance for vigorous exercise.

Ability to recover from physical activity:

- There are extremely accurate tests that can be done in the laboratory to study the condition of your heart and lungs, including your heart output, reaction time, oxygen debt, and maximum oxygen intake. The Harvard step test is a relatively easy test of your body's ability to recover from physical activity. It doesn't require any fancy equipment. You simply step up and down from a bench or block at a rate of 30 times a minute for 4 minutes. The height of the step or block used depends on your height.

Height of bench or block (inches)	Height of participant (feet and inches)
12	less than 5'0"
14	5'0"–5'3"
16	5'3"–5'9"
18	5'9"–6'0"
20	over 6'0"

After stepping up and down from the bench or block 120 times in 4 minutes, wait 1 minute. Then take your pulse for 30 seconds. Two minutes after exercising, take your pulse again for 30 seconds. Finally, 3 minutes after exercising, take your pulse once more for 30 seconds. You can now calculate your recovery index, which indicates how well your heart recovers from exercise.

$$\text{Recovery index} = \frac{\text{Duration of exercise in seconds x 100}}{\text{Sum of pulses x 2}}$$

Suppose your results were the following:

Minutes after exercising	Pulses felt in 30 seconds
1	45
2	40
3	35

Your recovery index would be calculated as follows:

$$\text{Recovery index} = \frac{240 \text{ seconds x } 100}{(45 + 40 + 35) \text{ x } 2} = \frac{24{,}000}{120 \text{ x } 2} = \frac{24{,}000}{240} = 100$$

86

Your recovery index would equal 100, which is excellent, as Table 10 shows.

Table 10: Physical Condition Based on Recovery Index

Physical condition	Recovery Index
Excellent	over 80
Good	65–80
Fair	50–65
Poor	less than 50

Moderate exercise endurance (see Table 11):

- Run and/or walk for 1.5 miles. Make sure you pace yourself and only do this test if you have been regularly participating in some type of physical activity.

Table 11: Endurance Levels for 1.5-Mile Run or Walk

Endurance Level	Time in minutes to run/walk 1.5 miles	
	Adolescent boys	Adolescent girls
Excellent	10.5 or less	11.5 or less
Good	10.5–11.5	11.5–12.5
Average	11.5–13.5	12.5–15.5
Fair	13.5–16.0	15.5–17.5
Poor	more than 16.0	more than 17.5

Aerobic and Anaerobic Exercise

Physical exercise is either aerobic or anaerobic, though some activities combine both. Anaerobic—without oxygen—exercise is short in duration and high in intensity. Aerobic—with oxygen—exercise is long in duration and lower in intensity.

Running to catch a bus, lifting a heavy weight, or sprinting 100 yards are anaerobic activities. Such activity requires short bursts of high energy, often without breathing. During anaerobic exercise oxygen is not used to provide the energy needed. Only limited amounts of energy can be produced in the absence of oxygen. Consequently, anaerobic exercise can occur for only short periods. The higher the intensity of the activity, the shorter its duration. The body can use anaerobic energy sources for one second to three minutes. After that time, muscles use aerobic energy, which requires oxygen.

As mentioned before, lactic acid is produced during anaerobic exercise. Its accumulation causes muscle fatigue. This is why lifting heavy weights or running full speed can only be done for a short time. After anaerobic activities, such as the 100-, 200-, or 400-meter sprints, 100-meter swimming events, gymnastics routines, football, volleyball, and weight lifting, athletes breathe heavily for some time. They have incurred what is known as an oxygen debt. The anaerobic exercise has left them with excess lactic acid. Their bodies respond by drawing more air into their lungs. The acid is then removed by reacting with the oxygen that enters their lungs and then their blood. When you exercise anaerobically, you tire faster and are more likely to have sore muscles after you stop.

For any activity that lasts more than two or three minutes, aerobic energy sources are needed. After the chemicals used for anaerobic energy are consumed, the aerobic sources, which require oxygen, must supply the muscles with energy. The oxygen reacts with a carbohydrate to release energy. For very long exercise sessions, the carbohydrate supply may be used up and fats or proteins will then be used to provide energy. Aerobic energy is more plentiful than anaerobic energy, and because lactic acid is not a substantial by-product of aerobic activity, it can go on for long periods of time. Eventually, the body does become tired from other factors, such as fuel depletion or dehydration.

Aerobic exercise conditions the heart and lungs. Working muscles need oxygen, so the body responds by drawing more air into the lungs. The heart beats harder and more efficiently, sending more oxygen-rich blood to the muscles. A stronger heart that contracts more forcefully and with fewer beats can deliver blood to the rest of the body more efficiently. A body with a stronger heart can do more work and exercise. The increased capacity for exercise benefits athletes and people engaged in fitness activities.

Aerobic activities include walking, jogging, swimming, aerobic dance, and skipping rope. Sports considered aerobic include cross-country skiing and running, and basketball. Aerobics can be defined as the use of large muscle groups for at least 15 to 20 minutes while maintaining 60 to 85 percent of the body's maximum heart rate.

Many sports commonly considered to be aerobic, such as tennis and basketball, also have an anaerobic component. These activities require periodic vigorous bursts of action. Anaerobic training along with the regular aerobic training for these sports help the athletes endure fatigue. Even athletes in cross-country running can benefit from anaerobic training. A fast start or a sprint at the end of a race requires anaerobic energy. Anaerobic training can help prepare an athlete for these and similar circumstances.

7-2*
The Effect of Aerobic Exercise on Heart Rate and Performance

Things you will need:

- clock or watch with a second hand
- notebook and pen or pencil
- volunteers of different ages, weights, and gender

Choose a type of aerobic exercise you enjoy doing—brisk walking, swimming, cross-country skiing, jogging, in-line skating, or bicycling. Do not use a competitive sport in your project because competition can increase stress and change your heart rate.

Take the tests included in Experiment 7-1 or take the President's Physical Fitness Challenge. Before you begin any exercise session make sure you warm up and stretch your body to help prevent injury. Be sure to cool down after exercising. (See Chapter 2.)

After warm-up and stretching, do your enjoyable aerobic exercise for 30 minutes three to four times a week. To make sure you are working aerobically during your exercise, take your pulse at least once during the activity. For aerobic exercise, your heart rate should be 60 to 85 percent of your maximum heart rate, which is 220 minus your age. Therefore, a 15 year old would have an aerobic heart rate of approximately 123 to 174.

$$220 - 15 = 205; \text{ and } 0.60 \times 205 = 123; 0.85 \times 205 = 174$$

You can check to see if you are at your target aerobic heart rate during exercise by stopping briefly to take your pulse for 10 seconds and multiplying by 6. Another simple but less accurate way to tell if you are working aerobically is your ability to talk while exercising. You should be able to carry on a short conversation while doing aerobic exercise. If you are gasping for breath while talking, you are probably working anaerobically.

Take your pulse before participating in the exercise and as soon as you finish. Also, take your pulse 30 minutes after exercising.

Record your results over a period of at least six weeks. What are your three pulse rates (before, immediately following, and 30 minutes following exercise) after completing six weeks of aerobic exercise sessions? How do these rates compare to the same rates when you first started this project? What physical condition were you in before conducting this project? Check your results on the physical fitness tests (Experiment 7-1) after completing this exercise project. Did you improve your performance level on any of the tests? What could explain any changes you find?

Have a number of volunteers of different ages, weights, and gender do this experiment. Have them do the physical fitness tests before and after doing this experiment. How does six weeks of aerobic exercise affect their ability to do the physical fitness tests? Does their physical fitness before the experiment affect the changes in any of their three heart rates (before, immediately following, and 30 minutes after exercise)?

Exploring on Your Own

Compare different types of aerobic activities. For example, do you work as hard while walking aerobically as you do while jogging? Test your pulse during these different activities. Compare other types of aerobic activities, like swimming or bicycling.

Try exercising at the high end of an aerobic activity (80 to 85 percent of your maximum heart rate) as compared to the lower end (60 to 65 percent of your maximum heart rate). How do your pulse rates at the two different levels compare? How much longer can you exercise at the lower level than at the higher level?

7-3
Anaerobic Exercise and Performance

Anaerobic exercise includes short periods of high intensity exercise, such as running, hopping, or skipping, separated by short periods of recovery time. It involves exercising at or near your maximum heart rate. The recovery rest period is slow jogging or walking. Remember to take into consideration your physical condition when you begin this experiment.

Things you will need:

• clock or watch with a second hand

• notebook and pen or pencil

• jump rope

Take the tests included in Experiment 7-1 or take the President's Physical Fitness Challenge. Before you begin any exercise session make sure you warm up and stretch your body to help prevent injury. Be sure to cool down after exercising. (See Chapter 2.)

Take your pulse before you begin to warm up, at least once during the exercise session to make sure you are working anaerobically, and immediately after exercising. Then take your pulse 30 minutes after exercising. During anaerobic exercise, you should be working at over 85 percent of your maximum heart rate.

The anaerobic exercise can be done for 10, 20, or 30 seconds (choose one) by running, hopping, or jumping rope as fast as you can. If you run for 10 seconds, rest for 10 seconds. Repeat 20 times. If you decide to run, hop, or jump rope for 20 seconds, rest for 15 seconds and repeat the series 10 times. If you decide on exercising for 30 seconds, rest 1 minute and repeat the series 8 times.

For longer times of anaerobic exercise, run hard for 1 minute, rest for 4 minutes and repeat the series 5 times. Or exercise hard for 2 minutes, rest for 10 minutes and repeat the series 4 times.

Compare your pulse rates after doing the exercise regimen 3 to 4 times a week for 6 to 8 weeks. Take the same tests you took at the beginning of your project and compare your results. Did the anaerobic training affect your results in any of the tests? Are you surprised? Were you in good anaerobic condition when you began the training project? Do you think that could have an effect on your results?

7-4
Performance After Aerobic and Anaerobic Training

Have one group of volunteers exercise aerobically for 6 to 8 weeks as suggested in Experiment 7-3. Have them take the tests of physical condition in Experiment 7-1 or have them take the President's Physical Fitness Challenge before and after the exercise regimen.

Have a comparable group work out anaerobically for 6 to 8 weeks 3 to 4 times a week as suggested in Experiment 7-3. Give the same tests and compare results.

Does one type of training appear to be better than the other for certain aspects of physical condition?

7-5*
Conditioning and Vital Capacity

The oxygen that the muscles of our bodies need in order to function is obtained from the air we breathe into our lungs. The more air we can breathe, the greater the amount of oxygen that can reach our blood and be carried to muscles and other tissues.

The volume of air we breathe can be measured with a device known as a spirometer (See Figure 25). You probably don't have access to a spirometer; but reasonably accurate measurements can be made with a plastic bag and a pail of water or with a one-gallon water-filled container and a piece of rubber tubing.

The volume of air you normally inhale and exhale is called your *tidal air*. The extra air you can inhale if you take a deep breath following a normal breath is called your *complemental air*. The volume of air you can force from your lungs after exhaling normally is called your *supplemental air*. After you have forced the supplemental air from

Things you will need:

- stethoscope
- a partner
- 2 large, rigid, transparent or semitransparent plastic containers, one with a volume of 1 gal, another about twice as large
- a glass or plastic plate large enough to cover the mouths of both containers
- dish pan
- tape
- marking pen
- large graduated cylinder or measuring cup
- 1-L or 1-qt plastic bag
- 12-inch length of rubber tubing
- a short length of glass or rigid plastic tubing
- cotton gauze or cotton balls
- rubbing alcohol
- twistie
- clock or watch with second hand
- calculator (optional)
- notebook and pen or pencil
- 2-L or 2-qt plastic bag
- 5–8-L or 2-gal plastic bag
- several volunteers of different ages, gender, heights, weights, and chest sizes

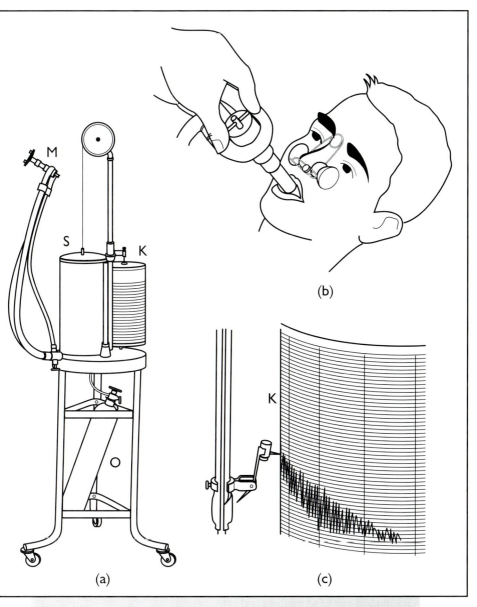

Figure 25. a) A drawing of a spirometer. M is the mouth piece; S is the spirometer bell; K is the kymograph where the volume of air inhaled and exhaled is recorded; O is the oxygen tank, which can be used to measure the volume of oxygen used by a subject. b) The part of the spirometer that fits into a person's mouth. c) A view of a record being made on the kymograph.

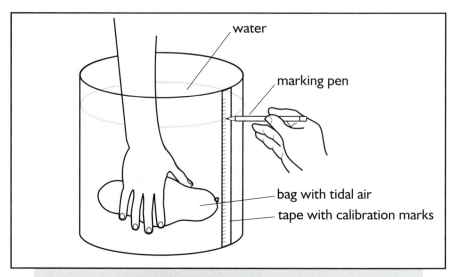

Figure 26. Measuring the volume of tidal air.

your lungs about one liter (1.1 quarts) of *residual air* remains in your lungs.

To measure your tidal air, calibrate a large (1-gallon or 4-liter) rigid, transparent or semitransparent plastic container. To calibrate it, first place a strip of narrow tape vertically along the side of the container. Then pour known volumes of water into the container and mark the water levels of the different volumes with a marking pen.

Pour some water into the container until the level is on one of the lines you marked. Hold your nose so that all the air you breathe goes through your mouth. When you have adjusted to mouth breathing, place the opening of a 1-liter or 1-quart plastic bag (from which all the air has been removed) firmly around your mouth just before you exhale. Collect the exhaled air in the bag. (Do not blow, just exhale in a normal way.) Twist the neck of the bag to seal off the exhaled air, and secure it with a twistie. **Caution: Never pull a plastic bag over your head.**

Hold the bag of air in your hand and push it under the water in the calibrated container as shown in Figure 26. Have a partner use a felt pen to mark the water level in the container before and after submerging the bag. Also mark your wrist at the water level. Finally, squeeze all the air out of the bag, hold the bag in your fist, put your fist back into the water up to the mark on your wrist, and have your partner mark the water level again. What is the volume of your hand and the empty bag? What is the volume of your tidal air?

Supplemental Air

To measure the volume of your supplemental air, completely fill the 1-gallon container with water. Cover the mouth of the container with a glass or plastic plate. Next turn the container upside down and place its neck under the water in a dish pan that rests in a kitchen sink. (See Figure 27.)

Insert a short length of glass or rigid plastic tubing into a 30-cm (12-in) length of rubber tubing. Use a piece of cotton gauze to wipe the end of the glass or plastic tube with rubbing alcohol. This tube will serve as a mouth piece. Once the alcohol has evaporated, have a partner support the water-filled container while you place the end of the rubber tubing up through the submerged mouth of the

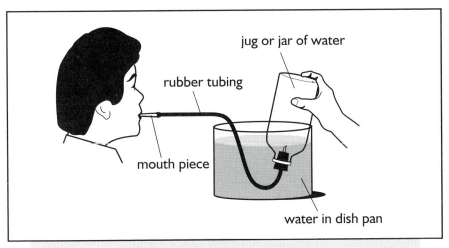

Figure 27. Measuring supplemental air.

container. Hold the mouth piece with your thumb and fingers as you breathe normally. After exhaling normally, force as much air as possible from your lungs through the mouth piece and rubber tubing and into the container. The supplemental air from your lungs will replace water from the container into the dish pan. When you have forcibly exhaled as much air as possible, pinch the rubber tubing with your fingers and remove it from the container.

Have your partner cover the submerged mouth of the partially filled container, remove it from the pan, and turn it upright. You can then use a graduated cylinder or measuring cup to measure the volume of water needed to fill the container. This is, of course, equal to the volume of air—your supplemental air—that you blew into the container. What is the volume of your supplemental air?

Vital Capacity

A person's vital capacity is the volume of air that he or she can forcibly exhale after taking the deepest inhalation possible. You can determine your vital capacity with the same equipment you used to measure your supplemental air.

Again, clean the mouth piece with gauze moistened with alcohol while your partner fills the 2-gallon container with water and places it in the dish pan. Place the end of the rubber tube through the submerged mouth of the container. Now, inhale as much air as you possibly can. Then exhale as much air as you can through the mouth piece and into the container. Once you have exhaled as much air as possible, pinch the rubber tubing and remove it from the container. Your partner will cover the submerged mouth of the partially filled container, remove it from the pan and turn it upright. You can then use a graduated cylinder or measuring cup to measure the volume of water needed to fill the container. What is your vital capacity?

Repeat the experiment to find your partner's vital capacity.

Show that a person's vital capacity is the sum of his or her complemental, tidal, and supplemental airs.

From all your measurements, what is the maximum volume of air that your lungs can hold? (Don't forget the one liter of residual air.) What is the maximum volume of air that your partner's lungs can hold?

Compare the vital capacities of a number of volunteers. Are these volumes related to age? To gender? To height or weight? To chest size?

Compare the vital capacities of a number of volunteers who are in good physical condition (as determined by the tests of physical condition in Experiment 7-1) with the vital capacities of people of comparable size, age, and gender who are not in good physical condition. Is vital capacity related to a person's physical condition?

Exploring on Your Own

How can you calculate the volume of air you breathe in one day?

How did scientists determine the volume of residual air? Is it related to a person's size?

Design and conduct experiments to determine the effect of smoking on vital capacity. Does smoking have any effect on tidal air? On supplemental air? On complemental air?

8

Sports Psychology

Sports psychology is the study of the relationship between the mind and sports performance. Sports psychologists help train professional and Olympic athletes. Many athletes believe the mind is as important to athletic performance as the body. Athletes need physical skills, but they also must be in the right frame of mind to perform at their best. What that frame of mind is depends on the sport. In sports such as baseball, tennis, or softball, players should be relaxed. Tenseness will hinder the smooth motor coordination needed for these games. On the other hand, football players need to be "psyched" for games. Their tenseness "explodes" in bursts of physical action.

Your mind can be a powerful means for improving your athletic performance. If you have ever played a competitive sport, you know what it is to "choke," to be so anxious that you perform below your normal level of ability. Choking occurs when anxiety causes you to pay attention to movements that are normally automatic. If you consciously attend to every little movement, they will not be fluid. Consider hitting a golf ball. If you are thinking about every movement of your arms, shoulders, wrists, hips, legs, and feet, you will disrupt the smooth swing that you are trying to perform to hit the ball well.

Your mind can also hinder your play if you cannot concentrate. You may be hearing spectator comments, or the other team may be intimidating you. No matter how good your skills are, if your mind is not focused on the game, you can lose. Think about a team that is undefeated and physically stronger than a weaker team. If the superior team feels complacent, the weaker team has a chance of winning. The weaker team has nothing to lose. If they do their best and the superior team does not concentrate on the game, the weaker team may win.

Basically, sport psychologists help athletes deal with the stress involved in sports. You can use some of their techniques to help your own or others' sport performance.

8-1*
Stress Management

Stress is part of life. There is "good" stress and "bad" stress. Examples of good stress are going to a prom or going on vacation. Good stress produces anticipation and the feeling of

Things you will need:

• stopwatch or watch with a second hand

• notebook and pencil or pen

• several volunteers

"butterflies" in your stomach. Examples of bad stress might include realizing you have too much work to do in too little time, or anticipating a big test in your least favorite subject when you don't understand the material. Bad stress causes fear and anxiety. When a person feels stress, the brain puts the body on full alert. The body increases its production of the stress-related hormones adrenaline and cortisol. The heart beats faster, the muscles become tense, and the body fills with chemicals that control pain and increase endurance. The pupils of the eyes dilate and hearing becomes more acute.

Response to stress has been a part of being human for a long time. It evolved in prehistoric times when our ancestors had to react to unexpected physical threats, such as an approaching woolly mammoth or large carnivore. Today, the stress we deal with is different, but the body still responds in the same way. If we do not have a release for the stress, it can build up and make us sick. Some physical symptoms of stress are headache, muscle ache, upset stomach, high blood pressure, inability to sleep, and fatigue.

We may not be able to control some situations that cause stress, but we can control our physical reaction to them. Some scientists believe controlling the body's expression of stress will affect the person's mental and emotional state. Techniques that have been shown to help the body deal with stress include deep breathing, relaxation, and exercise. In this experiment you can test some of these techniques.

Deep Breathing

Take your pulse by placing two fingers on the inside of your wrist as shown in Figure 5. Take your pulse for 15 seconds and record the number of times your heart beats. Multiply this number by four to find your heart rate in beats per minute.

Now take a slow, deep breath through your nose. Take the breath from deep down so that your abdomen expands. The intake of air should take about 7 seconds. Slowly exhale that air through your mouth for the same length of time. Continue breathing this way for two minutes. Then take your pulse for 15 seconds and record the result. Is there any difference in your heart rate after breathing deeply?

Try doing this breathing exercise 10 times a day for a week and note any changes in your pulse. Better yet, continue the exercise for 6 weeks and keep a record of your pulses. How do you feel after breathing like this? Are you more relaxed?

Perhaps a teacher will let you teach this breathing exercise to your classmates. Ask them to record their heart rate before and after doing the breathing exercise for two minutes. Ask them to provide a written account of how they feel after doing the breathing exercise for a number of days or weeks.

Try doing this exercise before a big test. Does it make you feel more relaxed? How about other students; do they feel more relaxed after doing the breathing exercise? If your teacher agrees, have the students write their observations about the breathing exercise after taking a test.

You can ask your parents or siblings to participate in your experiment. Maybe your parents could practice the breathing exercise at work and see if they notice any difference in how they feel. Ask them to try the breathing exercise before doing something stressful or even when returning home after work.

Relaxation

Relaxation is another way to help the body cope with stress. Take and record your pulse as instructed in the deep breathing exercise. Then lie on the floor or sit in a comfortable chair. Contract or tighten the muscles in your left foot and hold the contraction for a count of 5. Slowly relax the muscles. Now tighten the calf muscles in your left leg and hold for a count of 5 and slowly relax them. Repeat with the thigh muscles in your left leg. Continue to tighten and release all the muscles on the left side of your body up to the left shoulder. Then do the same on the right side of your body. Finish by tightening all the muscles in your body including your face and neck. Hold for a count of 5 and then completely relax all your muscles and let your body "sink" into the floor or chair for 20 seconds. Take and record your pulse again. Is there any difference? How do you feel after doing the whole relaxation process? Do you feel more relaxed? How about doing it before going to sleep? Do you think you will fall asleep faster? Try it for a week and see. Write down your observations.

See if you can get your family to try this experiment. Perhaps a teacher will agree to let you try the experiment with your classmates.

Should you have them do the experiment at the beginning or at the end of a class? Have them record their observations about how they feel after completing the relaxation process. Do some people feel differently than others? If so, why might that be?

Exercise

In these experiments, the exercise will not be demanding, but if you design experiments of your own using more strenuous activities, be sure to consult a doctor first. **Before anyone participates in any type of vigorous physical exercise, he or she should check with a doctor.**

Exercise is another way to alleviate physical signs of stress. When you exercise, your muscles contract and relax. This releases tension and increases your metabolism. Exercise depletes the response-to-stress hormones that linger in your body and generates endorphins, your "feel good" hormones. Psychologists and doctors do not agree about what kind of exercise best relieves stress. You can develop your own ideas about the effects of exercise as you experiment.

Choose a type of aerobic exercise you enjoy doing, such as taking a brisk walk, swimming, cross-country skiing, or bicycling. You should not use a competitive sport in your experiment because that can increase stress. You should do your enjoyable aerobic exercise for at least twenty minutes three to four times a week.

Take your pulse before exercising and again immediately after you finish. Obviously, your pulse after the exercise session will be higher. Then take it again one hour after completing the session. Record your results for a week. Continue this schedule for at least 6 weeks. What changes, if any, do you see in your pulse, before, immediately following, and one hour after completing your exercise sessions? Record, too, how you feel before and after exercising.

Can you get others to help out with this experiment and take part in the same schedule of aerobic activity? You might have different people do different types of aerobic exercise. Does the type of exercise seem to be a factor in reducing stress? Is age a factor? Gender? Weight?

Exploring on Your Own

Develop your own relaxation exercises and see if they help you to relieve stress.

Does your blood pressure increase when you are stressed? Enlist a school nurse to help you with this experiment. Take your blood pressure when you feel stress and when you do not. Is there any significant difference? How about after you participate in one of the stress management procedures?

Learn to take your resting heart rate. Your resting heart rate is your pulse when you first awaken in the morning and haven't participated in any physical activity at all—not even a yawn! Is there any change in your resting heart rate after you participate in a stress management procedure for at least 6 weeks?

Do just the opposite of relaxation. Can you and others increase your heart rates by just thinking of a stressful or frightening situation? Have subjects take their pulses and record their heart rates. Then ask them to visualize a stressful experience. Don't tell them what experience to think about. Let them think of their own, because what is stressful for one person may not be so for another. Right after they have visualized their frightening experience, have them take their pulse rates again. Do their pulse rates change? If so, how do they change?

8-2
Visualization

Once you have learned to relax, you can use the technique of visualization to help improve your athletic skills. Visualization is another mental technique that helps athletes deal with stress and improve performance. In visualization athletes improve their skills and confidence through mental practice. They visualize the muscle actions involved in their sport.

Things you will need:
- quiet place to relax
- a partner
- videotape and camcorder
- television
- coach, parent, or an older competent competitor in your sport
- basketball
- basketball backboard and hoop
- volunteers who enjoy basketball

Most psychologists believe mental rehearsals can improve athletic skill and concentration. Once you learn to relax and concentrate, mental rehearsals will help you perfect a skill. Dr. Herbert Benson advocates a technique that might help you with concentration. Sit relaxed and repeat a key word from your sport such as "ball" or "puck" while trying to think of nothing else. The idea is to screen out all other thoughts. After performing this technique a number of times, you should be able to just say the key word and be able to achieve complete concentration.

This same technique can be used with the relaxation exercise. Just say the word "relax" as you relax each muscle. After doing the relaxation exercise a number of times, the word "relax" will be so strongly associated with the relaxed muscles that merely saying the word will be enough to bring about complete relaxation. An athlete who has learned this technique simply says the word "relax" when he or she feels muscle tension or "chokes."

Visualization involves creating a clear mental picture of yourself doing your sport in a positive way. You not only see the movement in your mind but you also feel the motions, smell the

107

grass, use every sense to make the imagined experience as real as possible.

To do this, you can have someone videotape you performing your sport. Watch yourself and have your coach help you with technique. Divide the sport into its component skills. Evaluate your ability in each skill with help from your coach, parent, or an older competent competitor in your sport. Try to capture on tape the "perfect" shot or move. Slow it down and watch your movements. When you think about your play, recall the good parts and forget the bad parts. Rehearse those good movements physically and mentally. Try it in slow motion. Can you perform it in your mind in slow motion with your eyes closed? Once you have the perfect images in your mind, repeat the visualization over and over again. Practice being positive, seeing yourself successfully performing the sport. You want to reinforce and ingrain in your nervous system the positive aspects of your performance. Subconsciously, the mental rehearsals will send nerve impulses to appropriate muscles. You can actually practice with your eyes closed and your body relaxed. Try it.

Experiments have shown that basketball players who practice shooting free throws while blindfolded and then with their eyes open, improve their shooting more quickly than those who always practice with eyes open. Shooting without seeing seems somehow to provide better muscle sense. Try it. Can you think of another sport skill that could be practiced blindfolded without being dangerous? If so, practice the skill with your eyes open and then blindfolded. Have someone at about the same skill level try the same thing with their eyes open the entire time. Compare the results between the two practice techniques.

Further Reading

Cooper, K. H. *Kid Fitness*. New York: Bantam Books, 1991.

Corbin, C. B., and R. Lindsey. *Concepts of Physical Fitness, 7th Edition*. Dubuque, Iowa: Wm C. Brown Publishers, 1991.

Gardner, Robert. *Health Science Projects About Anatomy and Physiology*. Berkeley Heights, N.J.: Enslow Publishers, Inc., 2001.

———. *Health Science Projects About Nutrition*. Berkeley Heights, N.J.: Enslow Publishers, Inc., 2001.

———. *Science Fair Projects—Planning, Presenting, Succeeding*. Springfield, N.J.: Enslow Publishers, Inc., 1999.

———. *Science Projects About the Human Body*. Hillside, N.J.: Enslow Publishers, Inc., 1993.

———. *The Young Athlete's Manual*. New York: Julian Messner, 1985.

Hoeger, W.W.K., and S. A. Hoeger. *Lifetime Physical Fitness and Wellness, 4th Edition*. Englewood, Colo.: Morton Publishing Company, 1995.

Karolides, N. J., and M. Karolides. *Focus on Fitness*. Santa Barbara, Calif.: ABC-CLIO, 1993.

Rombauer, Irma S., Marion Becker Rombauer, and Ethan Becker. *The Joy of Cooking*. New York: Scribner, 1997.

Stokes, R., and D. Trapp. *Aerobic Fitness for Everyone*. Winston Salem, N.C.: Hunter Textbooks, Inc., 1994.

Internet Addresses

Franklin Institute Science Museum
<http://sln.fi.edu/>

Guide to Doing Science Projects
<http://www.isd77.k12.mn.us/resources/cf/SciProjIntro.html>

Health: Human Anatomy/Physiology
<http://www.carnegielibrary.org/subject/homework/health.html>

Sport! Science @ The Exploratorium
<http://www.exploratorium.edu/sports/index.html>

Index